"Over the years we have had many guests in o[ur] home, but none quite like Marilyn Laszlo. He[r] spunk and humor are wrapped around a heart that, for decades, has beaten to one cadence: to obey the great commission among Papua New Guinea's Sepik Iwam people. Here is a remarkable story of spiritual passion and perseverance, made possible not by her extraordinary gifts, but by her simple reliance upon almighty God. By all means read Mission Possible . . . and be prepared to receive a mission of your own."

—Dr. and Mrs. Billy Graham

"Accounts about life in river basins that are flooded half of every year may be authentic or fascinating, but rarely both. This chronicle of Marilyn Laszlo's experience in Papua New Guinea is eminently both. In spite of her many hardships, she never lost sight of her God-given goal—the New Testament in the language of the people."

—Elaine Townsend,
wife/widow of Wycliffe Bible Translators founder
William Cameron Townsend ("Uncle Cam")

"Marilyn's dynamic relationship with Christ showed me that living daily in God's will takes you far beyond any self-imposed dream or boundaries. My visit in Hauna introduced me to brothers and sisters in Christ who showed me the simplicity of loving the Lord wholeheartedly. This book reflects Marilyn's love for her Lord and the Sepik Iwam people."

—Suzanne Strudwick,
Ladies Professional Golf Association
Tour Player

To Adrienne & Jason

MISSION POSSIBLE

Marilyn Laszlo

Trust Jesus
and follow
your dreams

Marilyn Laszlo

Tyndale House Publishers, Inc.
WHEATON, ILLINOIS

Library of Congress Cataloging-in-Publication Data

Laszlo, Marilyn.
    Mission possible / Marilyn Laszlo.
        p.   cm.
    ISBN 0-8423-3881-0
    1. Laszlo, Marilyn.   2. Missions, American—Papua New Guinea—Hauna Village—History—20th century.   3. Bible.   Iwam language—Versions.   4. Missionaries—United States—Biography.   5. Missionaries—Papua New Guinea—Biography.   6. Summer Institute of Linguistics. Papua New Guinea Branch—Biography.   I. Title.
BV3680.N52L375   1998
266'.0092—dc21
[b]   98-25029

Printed in the United States of America

04   03   02   01   00
9   8   7   6   5   4

Dedication

This book is gratefully dedicated to Dr. Kenneth Taylor in recognition of his tireless support of missions, specifically of Wycliffe Bible Translators, and for his lifelong dedication to idiomatic Bible translation, which has resulted in countless people hearing God's Word in their own language.

CONTENTS

Foreword
Acknowledgments
Introduction
Map

1 Death Wailing
2 A Hasty Retreat
3 Marriage or Missions?
4 Stadium Standoff
5 Women or Ghosts?
6 More Than Vowels and Consonants
7 Fourteen Boys and a Shaman
8 Thorn Cures
9 Crocodiles and Calculators
10 Airmail
11 Trichinosis for Jesus
12 Translation Turning Points
13 Spitters to Saints
14 We Don't Need Gas—God Is Enough
15 Shirley Surrenders
16 A Church with No Christians
17 No, I'm Not Quitting!
18 Sharing the Load
19 Calling On a Greater Power
20 Jude 25
21 Six Hauna Men in a Flying Canoe
22 The Word of God Will Last Forever
23 Hebrews Hall of Faith

Epilogue
About the Writer
About Wycliffe Bible Translators

FOREWORD

One of my favorite chapters in the Bible is Hebrews 11, where we read about heroes of faith who lived thousands of years ago. As you are about to discover, *Mission Possible* is a twentieth-century story of heroism for the gospel.

I first met Marilyn Laszlo nearly twenty years ago while traveling overseas with Bill Cristobal, my college roommate. He had told me about Marilyn and the Bible translation work she was doing in remote Hauna Village, along Papua New Guinea's great Sepik River—but nothing he told me quite prepared me for my encounter with her.

Hauna Village is reachable only by boat or aircraft. To step to the ground there is to step back in time in one of the most unexplored regions on earth. In fact, some say Hauna Village is within walking distance of the end of the world. It is a wild area of thick jungle and lush tropical beauty, filled with adventures and dangers not even Hollywood can adequately portray.

The colorful Sepik Iwam people who live there routinely kill crocodiles and wild boars with their handmade weapons. For generations, life for them has been short and hard, with those fortunate enough to survive infancy typically dying from injury or tropical disease before age forty. Just as smoke from cooking fires would hang thick over the heads of villagers, a cloud of spiritual darkness hung over their lives. Occult shamans ruled village life.

I could hardly believe that the person God sent to relate his love and share his gospel with them was the little woman from Indiana whom I met: five-foot-two-inch Marilyn Laszlo. Yet there she was—bright, energetic, and obviously much loved as she poured herself into translating Scripture into the previously uncodified language of the Sepik Iwam. Neither isolation, nor rats, nor deadly snakes, nor hepatitis, nor malaria, nor any number of other daunting challenges had deterred her from her mission—to make disciples for the Lord Jesus Christ among these decidedly unreached people.

As I came to learn, the story of how God had led her there and used her to reach across a language and culture gap wider than the Grand Canyon is truly heroic. It is also a testimony to the faithfulness of God in preparing the way for his servants, in sustaining them in the face of unimaginable difficulties, and in enabling them to do his will no matter how impossible it may seem.

In the pages that follow, you can read much of that story for yourself. I believe that you will be fascinated, amazed, gripped by what God has done through this gutsy Christian lady. I think her faith, her patience, and her brokenhearted passion for the lost will stir in you a greater desire to let God work through you. That's the effect Marilyn has had on me, at any rate.

And as you read, you may even sense the Lord saying to you the same thing he said to Marilyn years ago, the words that launched her on this incredible journey: "Trust Me." The question is, How will you respond?

Franklin Graham

ACKNOWLEDGMENTS

Dr. Kenneth Taylor and Dr. Wendell Hawley at Tyndale House have been supportive of Wycliffe Bible Translators in so many ways, and their assistance in the publishing of this book is greatly appreciated. Years ago when I was an employee of Tyndale House, I never dreamed that the first book I would write would be published there.

I am very grateful to Ken Anderson for all his research, the initial interviews with Marilyn, his rough drafts of several chapters, and his suggestions. It has been his dream for years to see a book chronicling the completion of the Sepik Iwam New Testament.

Special thanks need to go to several of my Wycliffe colleagues. Robin Thurman, director of the Papua New Guinea branch, willingly took the time from his full schedule to offer his editorial comments on the entire manuscript and checked it for accuracy. I am indebted to Barbara Colborn for her painstaking and insightful editing.

Thanks also to my friends Betty Wendland and Joy Seward for their input and editorial suggestions. I want to recognize Broadway Christian Church in Fort Wayne, Indiana, which made their fax machine and printer available when needed.

This whole project has blessed me with the opportunity to get to know Marilyn Laszlo better. Even though my fifteen years in Papua New Guinea overlapped some of the time Marilyn was there, our paths didn't cross enough for me to know her as I do now. My thanks to her for opening her heart to me so we could share this story. I'm thankful for her patience with me as she retold stories to make sure I was writing them accurately.

My husband, John, couldn't have been more involved. For months he meticulously edited everything I wrote, even those teetering piles of chapters filling our study that never made it into the book! He kept me and the house functioning during several weeks of stressful deadlines. Though last in this list, John deserves my biggest thanks.

Luci Brockway Tumas

jam as dugout canoes arrived. Makapobiya was a man of distinction, and his cherished son was being buried.

Marilyn and Judy joined the procession, careful not to cause a distraction on such a somber day. They eased into their canoe and made their way to the cemetery on the other side of the river.

Were they up to this? Marilyn wondered as they left their canoe and walked toward the gathering crowd.

"Yiubiyie!" shouted several village children. "Ghost!" In hours of discussions over many communal fires, most Hauna people had decided that these pale creatures were not humans but visiting spirits of departed ancestors.

Marilyn and Judy eventually worked their way to the front of the crowd and came into full view of the burial site, reaching the shallow grave just as Bopia's body was lowered into it.

Without waiting for the bearers to step fully away, Makapobiya and his wife plunged forward. Falling first to their knees, they toppled into the grave. Other family members joined them, among them the guardian uncle and aunt who had been as responsible for the boy as his parents.

"Ayee-oh! Ayee-oh!" everyone sobbed loudly.

The tree bark shroud had opened as it was lowered into the ground so the family could touch him one last time. Marilyn cautiously stepped closer. No one seemed to mind. But what she saw pierced her heart with horror, like a thrown spear. The "corpse" moved his hand across his chin. He was struggling for breath.

"He's alive!" Marilyn gasped. "Judy, what can we do?"

Sauperi, Hauna's paramount leader, arrived just then and stood somberly at the head of the grave. Marilyn stepped back in deference. Sauperi cut an imposing presence. A wild boar's tusk, trophy of a recent hunt, hung from a dried animal-skin string around his neck. Earrings fashioned from vine fragments, streaks of white paint on each arm, and a headband of feathers further set him apart from the other men. In his mouth he bit tightly on an unlit pipe, bartered from an Australian official who had visited Hauna years earlier.

Even more than Makapobiya, Sauperi was a man shown great respect, a wise man with unchallenged authority. He spoke to the clansmen with courtesy but with firmness, and they drew Makapobiya, his wife, and others out of the grave.

Marilyn and Judy watched in shocked silence as slats hewn from the boy's split canoe were placed across the top of the grave. Then attendants placed leaves over this initial covering. When the first shovel of dirt was thrown onto the leaves, however, Marilyn lost her poise.

Taking a step forward she cried, "Bopia's still alive! Your boy isn't dead! He moves; he breathes! That means life!"

Engrossed in grief, Makapobiya didn't respond. His gaze remained fixed on the burial proceedings.

Even if the mourners had understood Marilyn's words, the parents could not have possibly believed Bopia was still alive. The attending spitter the previous night had pronounced the moment when the boy's spirit had left his body. Bopia had neither spoken nor responded to words or touch. Burial was inevitable.

Marilyn turned toward Sauperi. It was he who had granted their initial request a few weeks earlier to live in Hauna. Speaking through an interpreter in the trade language—Melanesian Pidgin—Marilyn and Judy had explained that they wished to live in Hauna to observe and learn. It was Sauperi who had arranged housing until their own house could be built. Now, however, he stood like a totem, as if ignoring them.

"You can't bury that boy! He's alive!" Marilyn gestured toward the grave. "He's only in a coma! We have medicine that could help him. Please! Don't bury him!" In her panic she forgot she was speaking in English.

Slowly Sauperi turned toward Marilyn, his eyes drilling into the distraught visitor. Although he didn't understand English, he fully discerned the passionate intent of Marilyn's voice. Anger spread across Sauperi's face.

Marilyn began using Pidgin, *"Dispela pikinini em i gat laip!"* ("This child is alive!")

Sauperi stepped forward. He reprimanded her in his language, which she didn't understand, but his gestures, attitude, and intonation clearly conveyed his meaning. "You shut your mouth! You don't know anything!"

Marilyn's heart pounded.

Sauperi, the dominant leader, would be strategic in reaching these people. It was vital to remain on good terms with him. Had he just become an adversary?

Marilyn wilted. What had come over her? She was conducting herself exactly opposite from her training. She knew nothing of the cultural meanings here. She was an outsider, a stranger with zero rights to speak.

These gentle people had accepted her as a friend. The men respected her and Judy and would protect them as faithfully as they would the women of their own clan. Now she had insulted them in their time of anguish.

Overwhelmed with frustration, she rejoined Judy.

Villagers continued to throw dirt onto the canoe slats and leaves. No dirt would touch the body. Many months later, Makapobiya's wife would come and retrieve the skull and then carry it with her, to help her feel close to her son.

"Why are they burying him alive?" Marilyn couldn't resist asking Judy. "If he can move and breathe, he's not dead."

As they started to walk away, Marilyn stopped abruptly. Looking back, she saw the mourners in renewed travail with friends supporting and consoling them as they left the graveside. She took a step as if to return to them, but Judy restrained her.

"We've got to get down to him, Judy! We just can't leave him there to smother and die. One injection might save his life!"

She looked alternately at Sauperi and back toward the grave. The mound of earth lay in symbolic terror against the hillside. It was like a scene from some horror movie, only there was no director to call "Cut!" A living boy lay beneath that cruel mound.

The chief's eyes remained stern, judicial. He held the scepter of authority for Hauna. This had been the accepted custom of burial, practiced by generations long preceding him. The boy had been properly pronounced dead. Sauperi was responsible for what happened here.

Dare she defy the great man?

A plan formed in her mind. She would stand her ground until Sauperi walked away. Then, in moments, she could fetch the medical kit. Given a half hour, even with bare hands, she could perhaps dig back into the grave to save Bopia!

As though he read her thoughts, Sauperi stood like a sentinel.

Marilyn wanted to cry out to him, "We don't want to cause a problem here; we're here to help you. You know the meaning of human love. We want to share the message of God's love."

Unable to speak his language, she could only stand in awkward, demeaning silence. As shaman and translator stood eyeball-to-eyeball, time seemed to stand still.

Finally, Marilyn lowered her gaze. She and Judy shuffled back toward their canoe.

"Oh, Marilyn, I can't believe this! How will we ever get through to these people?"

"I don't know, Judy. This is beyond me. Only God can help us."

THREE

Marriage or Missions?

*All Marilyn had to do was to tell Don
she would skip the missions idea.*

Growing up on an Indiana farm, Marilyn was immersed in
the folklore and philosophy of her Hungarian-born grandfa-
ther. Grandpa Laszlo, with his grandiose well-groomed
mustache, was like someone cut out of a storybook.

Since the Laszlos had no son, Marilyn worked at her
father's side in the fields. As a young child she would sit on
his lap for rides around the farm. Grandpa worked with
horses, but Daddy preferred the tractor, and as Marilyn
grew, he taught her how to operate it by herself.

Her three younger sisters were all charmingly feminine,
playing with their dolls or dressing up in their mother's
clothes. But when she wasn't helping her father, Marilyn,
ever the energetic tomboy, would insist that the girls play
cops and robbers or cowboys and rustlers, with big sister
always portraying one of the bad guys.

Marilyn seemed to have a knack for getting into trouble.
One day, along with her sister Shirley and their cousin, she

gathered some abandoned cigarette butts. After stealing matches from the kitchen, the girls sneaked off behind Grandpa Laszlo's large outdoor haystack. When they heard Grandpa coming, they hid the smoldering butts behind their backs. Unfortunately, the still glowing cigarettes touched the hay behind them, and as the three culprits ran in different directions, Grandpa's winter's store of animal roughage went up in blazing smoke!

Childlike faith in God came as naturally to Marilyn as did her ability to throw a softball from third to first base or to sink a hook shot from the corner. She loved sitting in the front row of Crocker Bible Church, a one-room country school building made over to accommodate farmers for Sunday worship. It was here that a visiting missionary to Russia described modern Christian heroes living under communism. A missionary from the Yucatan Peninsula once said, "Mexico is our near neighbor, like the family next door, and yet we give these people little attention."

One day while driving the tractor, twelve-year-old Marilyn looked heavenward and called out, "When I'm grown up, Lord, I wonder if I could be a missionary and go some place where people have never heard about Jesus."

Realizing that she needed to trust Jesus for the forgiveness of her sins, Marilyn made a public confession of her faith at a Billy Graham Crusade and began the challenging adventure of allowing Jesus Christ to be the Lord of her life. Feeling that she was always in trouble for something, she sensed the need to take a public stand to confess her faith so everyone knew she really meant it.

As she blossomed into adolescence, boys seemed to find her attractive, although she became best known as the girl you'd like to have on your team.

Discontentment flickered in her mind after she graduated

from high school. She went through the next four years wondering if her restlessness came from a failure to surrender herself entirely to God's will for her life. She shifted from job to job: strawberry picker, factory worker, file clerk, secretary, and doctor's office receptionist.

Throughout her teens and early twenties, Marilyn dated a string of respected, athletic, and fun young men. Then romance budded with a handsome basketball and football star. They had great times together, going to ball games and sharing activities at church.

One moonlit night as the couple sat parked at the Laszlo farmstead, Marilyn began to worry that a proposal might be coming. In that moment she recalled her prayer many years before on a tractor. She thought of the years since high school and how pointless her life seemed. As she studied the young man's face, she also realized how deeply she wanted to encourage his proposal. Instead, she bid him a friendly good-night, got out of the car, and walked quickly into the house. The following months brought an emotionally painful drifting apart as they both sensed God leading them in different directions.

Marilyn's pastor had seen her restlessness and struggles and had been praying for her. Drawing her aside one day, he asked, "You have so much talent, Marilyn. Have you thought about college?"

Her parents' initial reaction to the suggestion was, "No Laszlo has ever gone to college." But that year's corn crop income went to pay Marilyn's tuition and expenses at Bryan College in Dayton, Tennessee.

Majoring in history, music, and Bible, she also earned a considerable reputation as a competitor in women's athletics. In her junior year she also wore the coveted crown of Homecoming Queen. She still dreamed about being a missionary, but her basketball jump shots, her .300 softball batting average, and her track speeds all persuaded guidance counselors to encourage her to focus her future toward a teaching and coaching career.

After graduating, Marilyn put missionary service in the background as she taught school for four years near her hometown of Valparaiso, Indiana. While paying off school bills with her day job, she earned a master's degree in education and psychology at Indiana University. It seemed evident that God was going to use Marilyn to minister to young people.

A white Ford Galaxy XL convertible—a dream come true!

Top down and radio blaring, Marilyn's car attracted students like a magnet the first time she pulled into the school parking lot. Boys jumped into the backseat. Girls ran their fingers along the upholstery.

"How many banks y'gotta rob to buy yourself wheels like this?" a senior boy wanted to know.

"Can ya pop the hood t'show us how many horses ya got?"

Over the next five years as a teacher, girls' athletic director, and counselor, she had many opportunities to share her faith. She remained involved at church by teaching Sunday school and spearheading youth activities.

However, Jeremiah 29:11 had caught her attention, and she began quoting it often: "'For I know the plans that I have for you,' declares the Lord, 'plans for welfare and not for calamity to give you a future and a hope.'"

Plans? Future? Once when talking with an alto seated next to her in the church choir, Marilyn confided that she wanted to become a missionary.

"Oh, Marilyn, forget it!" the woman said. "You're not the missionary type!"

Since she respected her friend's evaluation, Marilyn didn't pursue missions for at least two more years.

Then one night she was jolted awake by what she felt was a voice from heaven. The Lord seemed to be saying: "Marilyn, you promised me when you were a young girl that you would go to the mission field if I called you. I'm calling you now."

No longer doubting the call, she nevertheless had a practical problem to face. *Lord, you know that I've accumulated some debts,* she prayed. *I can't leave these to my family. If you'll just give me time to pay off these debts, I'll fulfill my promise.*

In a matter of days she lined up a better paying teaching post in Marquette, Michigan. With her belongings in her Ford convertible, she headed north with the top down all the way beyond the Straits of Mackinac to the brisk shores of Lake Superior. Since her teacher's salary would not reduce her debts quickly, she moonlighted making hamburgers and waitressing, working from five until midnight. As a result, she paid off all her debts within one year and had some money left over.

Teaching that year went exceptionally well. The convertible augmented her rapport with the students. After school, even on bitterly cold days, she often found a half dozen students huddled around her snow-colored wonder in the parking lot.

"Put the top down," one of them would urge. Marilyn always complied.

One afternoon as the sunset painted the snow, ice, and water into a wonderland of pink, Marilyn parked the convertible alongside Lake Superior and watched nightfall settle. Her life had taken many steps from the poor little

Indiana farm girl to the prestigious, young high school teacher.

"Lord, I know there are great highways in Mexico," she prayed aloud. "Don't you think I should keep this car as a missionary and drive it to Mexico?"

And there were other emotions to analyze that afternoon. Don Daniels had returned home from his stint in the navy. He was superbly handsome and a dynamic Christian with a recording-quality baritone voice. He had caught sight of Marilyn at the same moment she had caught sight of him! Soon they were singing duets in church, and together they helped spark the church's youth society.

If she had placed an order in heaven itself, she couldn't have found someone more suited to her requirements for a husband! Don was warm-hearted, an invigorating conversationalist, and as morally astute as one of the apostles.

Inevitably they took lakeshore drives in Marilyn's convertible.

As the pair grew closer and closer, Marilyn realized that she needed to be honest with Don and tell him about her goal to be a missionary. One night, by her design, they dined at a Mexican restaurant, where she introduced him to chimichangas.

"I've never been all that crazy about Mexican food," Don said, "but that's because I never dated anyone who knew what to order."

"Mexican food's my favorite."

"Ever been to Mexico?" he asked.

"Not yet."

"Good place to visit together," Don suggested.

She felt her cheeks redden.

"Never been there myself," Don continued when the silence grew awkward. "A friend of mine was impressed with the university in Mexico City. Beautiful campus, he told me, with an Aztec motif for all the buildings."

"My interest is in the jungles," Marilyn said candidly.

"Jungles?" Don exclaimed. "I thought women were allergic to bugs and snakes."

She told him about the missionaries who had spoken at her church, especially the woman who had worked among Indians in the Mexican jungles.

"So you want to be a missionary there yourself?"

Marilyn nodded. "Am I foolish thinking about being a missionary in Mexico?" she asked.

He hesitated, then slowly shook his head. "No, that's admirable." His eyes affirmed the sincerity of his response.

"How about you, Don?"

"Become a missionary?"

She nodded, adding, "I bet you'd sound great singing in Spanish."

Now *his* cheeks reddened.

"Y'know," he said, "maybe I would like being a missionary." Marilyn's heart skipped a beat. "Couldn't be any worse than the navy."

They finished eating, and Don became reflective. "You and I can talk about missions," he sighed, "only for me—it'd never work."

"Why not?"

"It just wouldn't." He motioned to the waiter for the bill. "Nope."

As they sat beside the lake that night, Don fidgeted. He tenderly took Marilyn's hand and clasped it tightly.

"Commitment is an awesome thing, Marilyn. When I was in the navy, I was committed to the navy. Before I went in, I took a new step in my Christian life. I asked God to make me a better person through the experience. I committed myself to keeping clean. No drugs. No liquor. No port women."

The grip of their hands tightened.

"I was able to handle the temptations," he continued, "since I'd already decided what my responses would be."

Tears came to Marilyn's eyes. She couldn't suppress them. What an incredible missionary this guy could become!

"I commend you for your interest in Mexico," he continued. "I hope it all works out for the best. But, y'know, if it doesn't . . . if Mexico doesn't pan out . . . I've thought of asking you to marry me. But," he cleared his throat, "I know I could never make it on the mission field."

All Marilyn had to do was to tell Don she would skip the missions idea. But she *knew* God's plan for her future involved missions. She chose to be obedient to his plan, even if she had to follow as a single woman.

FOUR

Stadium Standoff

*"Look, Lord," Marilyn prayed, "I gave up teaching, sold that
beautiful convertible. What more do you want?"*

"'For I know the plans that I have for you,' declares the
Lord, 'plans for welfare and not for calamity to give you a
future and a hope.'"

This promise from Jeremiah 29:11 took preeminence in
Marilyn's thinking and prayers. She didn't expect God to
send an angel to deliver a blueprint, yet she did believe God
wanted to reveal his plans for her.

Feelings toward Don lingered. What a husband he would
have been. She had always presumed marriage to be in
God's plan for her. With each year of teaching, her love for
young people deepened, and her expertise in relating to
them grew. But Marilyn repeatedly took refuge in the Jeremiah verse.

One mild winter Saturday she took a long drive with the
top down and the heater on full blast. Wending her way
along Lake Superior's shoreline, she came to the place where
she and Don had had their definitive moment.

Lord, she prayed, *why couldn't Don and I have ministered together in Mexico? He would have been so helpful.*

Mexico. How was she ever to get there? She was struck with the realization that since she had made the break with Don, she now needed to discover which mission group she would join. She knew little about the numerous organizations, their needs, or what they offered.

Marilyn drove home and reviewed a sheaf of brochures she had collected from various groups. Excited to sense a clear direction, she wrote to five for further information and prayed for God's direction as she mailed the stack of letters, sensing the first reply might change her life.

The very first reply came from an organization she knew little about: Wycliffe Bible Translators. Along with a letter from Wycliffe was information describing the unique character of its worldwide mission. She was captivated by reports of the thousands of languages still unwritten and of the millions of people who had no chance to read God's Word for themselves.

Her interest caught fire when she learned that Wycliffe thoroughly trained their workers, then sent them to live among an ethnic group to learn the language, put it into written form, and teach the people to read and write it. The goal was to eventually translate the Scriptures with the people's help.

And Wycliffe had workers in the jungles of Mexico!

At that time Wycliffe required two summers of linguistic education for prospective translators. As Marilyn headed off to the University of Oklahoma for the Summer Institute of Linguistics (SIL) courses, she told everyone who would listen, "I'm going to be a Bible translator in Mexico."

She had notified God, too, so it was final.

Don was the most supportive, promising, "I'll pray for you every day."

She had hardly arrived on the Oklahoma campus when she *felt* rather than *heard* God's voice saying, "Not Mexico, Marilyn, but New Guinea."

Making up that voice was a set of curious circumstances. That summer, SIL was giving high priority to New Guinea, a South Pacific territory with over eight hundred languages yet to be reduced to writing. (In 1975 it became the independent nation of Papua New Guinea.) Because of this emphasis, several SIL faculty members were translators home on furlough from New Guinea. There were also many applicants training for service in New Guinea: Marilyn's roommate, her companions at the dining table, and several classmates.

The biographies of esteemed missionaries also influenced her: William Carey, George Grenfell, Adoniram Judson, and David Livingstone. She reveled in their dedication and courage, measuring her own willingness to sacrifice against theirs.

Of all the towering figures, she found herself attracted mostly to James Chalmers, who had served with the London Missionary Society. Chalmers's story, *Pioneering in New Guinea*, was regarded as a missionary classic, and his incredible courage presented Marilyn with a sobering challenge. She wept whenever she read and reread the account of that Easter morning in 1901 when, going up New Guinea's wild Fly River, Chalmers and a companion were attacked, beheaded, and eaten by cannibals.

Confused by the contrasting tugs between her long-time leanings toward Mexico and the thought that the Holy Spirit was leading her toward New Guinea, Marilyn plunged into depression.

The first item on the application form she was about to turn in stated: List your choices of countries. She had written:

First choice: Mexico
Second choice: Peru
Third choice: Colombia

"If you're sure God wants you in Mexico," her SIL counselor told her, "then that's where you should go. But please keep your options open to New Guinea."

Her plan on Friday morning was to drop off the application on the way to her first class, but there was more than an hour before class time. Still confused and depressed about submitting her choice of countries, she tossed the application onto her bed.

Since she had already bagged her laundry, she headed for the laundromat, taking along her Bible to read while she waited. When she found the place crowded and noisy, she swung her laundry bag over her shoulder and fled the boisterous scene.

The distress in her stomach intensified. She decided to skip classes and take some time to wrestle with the Mexico versus New Guinea conflict inside her.

In her search for a quiet place, she found the University of Oklahoma's sprawling football stadium, which was empty of all life since it was the off-season. Even the adjoining tennis courts were deserted. What place could be quieter or more conducive to prayer and sorting out troubled thoughts? Inspecting the twelve-foot-high fence topped with barbed wire, she noticed one of the tall gates stood narrowly ajar. On impulse, she went through the gate, shut it, and then climbed to the very top row of stadium seats.

She imagined the cheers on an autumn day from the sixty thousand fans. She could almost hear students yelling, "Mexico! Mexico!" while an opposite section cried out, "New Guinea! New Guinea!"

Mexico has two hundred languages waiting to be translated, she prayed. *So what's the big deal? New Guinea! I've hardly ever heard of the place! It's the end of the world! If you go any farther, you start coming back again. I need to be nearer to my parents. You say we're not to neglect our mothers and fathers. Look, Lord, I gave up teaching. I sold that beautiful convertible. What more do you want?*

I don't need your teacher's paycheck; I don't need that convertible. I need you, Marilyn, God seemed to impress upon her heart.

Frustrated, she tossed her laundry bag onto one of the bleachers, stretched out under the summer sun, and fell asleep.

She woke up very hungry about one o'clock. She had missed lunch, but she remembered a hamburger stand near the stadium. She hurried down to the gate.

Closed and locked!

All the other gates were padlocked, too, she discovered as she ran looking for some kind of exit.

"Isn't there anybody in here?" she called out. No one answered.

She returned to the top of the stadium and searched across the distant campus. She waved and called to anyone she saw. No one could hear her. The only person to come near enough to hear was a small boy on a bicycle. He looked up, then pedaled rapidly away as though he had seen a ghost.

Hunger the stadium inmate could tolerate. But long hours in the burning summer sun had left her dehydrated. She remembered seeing a drinking fountain, hurried to it, but found that the water had been turned off, apparently due to construction.

But nearby was a pop machine.

She selected coins intended for the laundry. But the machine was empty!

"Oh, well," she encouraged herself, "I can make it until morning."

Stadium mystique became all the more captivating as evening came. To fill in the long hours alone, she fantasized that she was attending a Billy Graham rally and that she was on the program as a soloist. She never imagined that one day she would be featured at one of the famed evangelist's crusades, but not for a solo!

Facing the bleachers from the turf at the fifty-yard line, she sang:

> *"Then sings my soul, my Savior God to thee,*
> *How great thou art! How great thou art!"*

Her imaginary audience clapped and whistled for an encore. Songleader Cliff Barrows smiled broadly and turned to vocalist George Beverly Shea, who nodded approval.

"You must come back again," she imagined Billy saying.

Before darkness settled, she arranged her laundry into a pillow and pulled a large bath towel over herself. She began another long talk with God. While pleading again for divine direction that would allow her to work in Mexico, she finally fell asleep.

A midnight cloudburst awakened Marilyn. Drenched, she grabbed her bag and sprinted down the cement stairs to find shelter beneath one of the ramps. But in her dash to escape the rain, she tripped and fell, bounding down a couple rows of steps, her bag of laundry tumbling behind. A sharp pain in her right leg caused her to fear a possible fracture. Although the deep wound bled, she found that she could walk. Dripping blood, she limped across the field toward a sheltered spot. In the darkness, however, she tripped over a water hose and fell into a puddle, adding mud to her blood-stained clothes.

At last under the shelter, feeling battered and exhausted, she again took up her miserable monologue with God. "Lord," she prayed out loud, "are you letting this happen to me to make me realize that your plan for me is not Mexico, which I've so stubbornly wanted?" She settled down on her soggy bag of laundry and tried to sleep again.

Saturday morning she went back to the top of the bleachers and watched her colleagues head off to breakfast, but no one saw her or heard her calling. She began to worry that if no one came that day, she'd probably have to wait two more days. This weekend was a special time of prayer with no classes, so her roommate probably wasn't even missing her.

Hungry, thirsty, and desperate, she knelt on the fifty-yard line and told God, "If you want me to go to New Guinea, here I am, Lord. I will go anywhere you want me to go—just get me out of this place!"

She might have remained a prisoner in the Oklahoma Sooners' stadium until Monday morning if a coach and his daughter had not come to an adjacent tennis court. After discovering the bedraggled captive, the coach found a key to the stadium gate.

To Marilyn, this crisis was a divine intervention. The scar on her leg reminded her of God's assurance that he would guide her.

FIVE

Women or Ghosts?

*It was determined that these visitors were neither male nor
female, but "its." They were spirits and not people.*

Eighteen months after her stadium incarceration, Marilyn
was in New Guinea. During the orientation period, she met
Judy Rehburg, and the two eventually decided to work
together. Both were anxious to live among a language group
with little previous outside contact. After studying survey
reports, they felt that the Sepik Iwam people, living on a
tributary off the vast Sepik River, were those whom God
wanted them to contact.

They needed to visit the Sepik Iwam people and ask per-
mission to live among them and learn their language. Taking provisions for a few days, they flew from Ukarumpa to
Ambunti, an airstrip and small outpost built next to the
Sepik River.

Neal Kooyers, another translator living on the Sepik,
piloted their dugout canoe, which was powered by an outboard motor. They traveled upriver for over 150 miles, visiting several Sepik Iwam villages. Sitting in the cramped

canoe for hours at a time over the four-day trip, the novices had plenty of time to study the flora and fauna.

Marilyn fell in love with the lush rain forest, home to many of New Guinea's unique birds with their dazzling rainbow plumage. Lining the river was foliage that would fascinate any florist back home.

This was the fabled Sepik River, one of the world's great waterways. It had been said by some to be more fearful than the Congo, and less explored than the Amazon. To travel its seven-hundred-mile length would be to journey back thousands of years, meeting people living exactly as they had lived for centuries. The trio chugged past villages built along the riverbanks, invariably stirring excitement among the local inhabitants.

Fear gripped Marilyn when the canoe became bogged down on a sandbank. Unable to move, the three travelers had to splash out into three feet of mud and push themselves back into deeper water, praying that there were no crocodiles nearby or that they were at least napping.

Her childhood prayer on the tractor was answered when at last they turned their canoe onto the tributary, and Hauna, one of the main Sepik Iwam villages, slid into view.

"This is Hauna!" Marilyn exclaimed. "We were told to look for a village with a hill in its middle."

Like most of the settlements on the Sepik, the houses stood in water six months out of the year. But unlike other villages they had visited, this one had a hilly area—about three acres of land—high and dry and unoccupied. An added feature was that the village was surrounded by distant mountains.

Neal cut the motor, and the canoe drifted toward the bank. Vine-belted men jumped into their canoes and soon surrounded the visitors. It seemed that the entire population called out to each other in excitement as they guided their guests into the village.

Without knowing a word of the Sepik Iwam language, the trio of visitors soon found themselves sitting on a log, attending a village-wide meeting.

"Husat i gat save long Tok Pisin?" Neal asked. ("Does anyone here speak Melanesian Pidgin?")

"Mi save liklik," one young man answered. ("I know a little.")

Several of the young men had worked on plantations downriver and had learned a bit of the regional trade language. They gathered around the guests to interpret. Eventually, by volleying Melanesian Pidgin back and forth, Neal was able to explain the reason for their presence: "These two women would like to come and live here and learn how to speak your language."

No one could understand why.

Their request was relayed to the village leaders, and a long, serious meeting followed. Marilyn and Judy would learn much later that it took the council the first half hour of the meeting to discuss what they were. It was determined that these visitors were neither male nor female, but "its." They were spirits and not people.

When that matter was settled, the essence of the discussion was passed along in sketchy Pidgin by the young men. After hours of conferring, a decision was finally reached. One of the village leaders pointed out that these creatures were white and obviously frail, therefore weaker specimens. "We are strong men," he declared, "of a strong people. What harm could they do? Wouldn't our enemies laugh at us if we showed ourselves to be afraid of them? There are only two of them and so many of us."

That argument convinced the others. After the vote was

taken, Sauperi, a venerable old leader of regal bearing, stood to speak. Sauperi announced the agreed-upon decision: Marilyn and Judy could come to live in Hauna.

Delighted, the two women thanked the council, promising to build a house. But they had another weighty question: Where could they build it? Worried about their ability to step out of a teetering canoe onto the stairs up to a house, they decided they would need dry ground for stability.

The village was already crowded with fifty-four large village houses, built on stilts to allow the seasonal high water to flow around them. House sizes ranged from fifty to eighty feet long, depending on how many brothers and their families occupied the house.

Noticing that the land on the hill was vacant, the visitors asked about the possibility of building there, in the middle of the village. The people recoiled. They explained that no one had built there because the land was actually an ancient cemetery. This hill belonged to Sauperi, who was not only the village's main leader but also its head shaman. From years of experience, he knew the ruckus the mountain spirits raised when even one tree was cut down.

During the ensuing village discussion, it was pointed out that if these visitors were indeed spirits, the hill would be the ideal location for the new house.

Gravely, Sauperi made his second announcement of the day: The visitors could build a house for themselves on his land.

They made plans for a house to be built on the allotted space. Three Wycliffe carpenters from Ukarumpa would need to spend three weeks in Hauna framing and finishing the house, using local materials for the bark floor and the thatched roof. Marilyn and Judy took up temporary residence in an empty village house that government agents used on their occasional visits.

On their first night in that borrowed house they were assaulted by swarms of vicious mosquitoes and flying ants. Hastily rigging up mosquito nets, they laid out woven grass mats on the uneven floor. They were joined by uninvited pests, who came right through the nets.

As they heard rats, lizards, and small pythons rustling in the roof thatch, they were surrounded by God's symphony of rain-forest night sounds: cries of wild birds, grunts of crocodiles, sounds of other night animals, insects, and bats. Meanwhile, king-sized cockroaches scampered across the floor and over the tops of their nets and, during the night, nibbled giant holes in the mosquito netting.

Daylight brought gentler adjustments, among them the laughter of little children who swarmed about, eager for further looks at the two "spirit" women with the white skin. Since their house provided little privacy, Marilyn and Judy were constantly on display. Daily life for the new linguists— the clothes they wore, the food they ate, brushing their teeth—seemed odd and amusing to the young observers.

Within their first month in the village, Makapobiya's son died. Marilyn and Judy witnessed his being buried alive and had fled in emotional trauma. Their weeks in Ukarumpa had been restorative, and now they were returning to Hauna.

Twinges of apprehension pricked Marilyn's heart. Her usual optimism was dulled. As she thumbed through her Bible, she read again the Jeremiah 29:11 promise.

The MAF pontoon plane circled Hauna village as a signal for the people to travel down their tributary to the broader Sepik River, where the flying canoe could land. Men standing and women sitting, an armada of dugout canoes skimmed toward the landing site. Pointing, waving, and calling to each other, they paddled thirty minutes to reach the aircraft. Villagers would discuss this experience over household fires for nights to come. What other village, up or down the Sepik, had visible spirits dwelling in their midst?

As Marilyn watched the enthusiastic Hauna greeting, she felt a twinge of guilt. She had heard of missionaries who lived where they were ignored or rejected by the locals. How often did a couple of newcomers enjoy this kind of initial reception?

O God, she prayed silently, *fill my heart with love. I'll fail if I try to do your work here on my own.*

At best, Marilyn and Judy were curious collector's items to enjoy and display. Some children ran to their mothers at the sight of these spirit creatures. Other youngsters found them to be more interesting than their usual pastimes. As the on-looking children returned to their homes and told what they had seen, adults with time to spare came to observe. Consequently, Judy and Marilyn had little privacy. Whatever they did, the gallery of spectators on the hillside was watching.

Judy and Marilyn did not have sufficient vocabulary to measure the impact of all the local commentary on their return. It took over a year before they learned what the people's initial impressions of them had been.

"They pay no shell money for the flying canoe's cargo."

"Whatever they want, the spirits give them. They do not need to work the way we do."

The flying canoe had brought back not only these pale-skinned creatures but also strange-shaped "baskets," card-board boxes. Canoes ferried those boxes to the shore, where a host of volunteers, those bold enough to touch items from the spirit world, carried the boxes to the translators' residence. As the boxes of supplies were placed at the base of the house, people came boldly to examine the wonders. Some lingered on the hillside, from where they had a clear view into the upper residence.

Conversations around the fires at night described the mysteries of the visiting spirits' canned food—each can appeared to be a hard, fruit-type object to Hauna eyes. The spirits opened these "fruits" and took out spirit-food. But where did they get such strange supplies? Villagers, who had an answer for everything, quickly solved the riddle. Since the white women were spirits, they could journey into the earth at night, under the burial mountain. There they met departed ancestors, who shared with Marilyn and Judy the fruit from wondrous trees unknown to mortals. These strange cans were actually "fruit" from such trees.

And then there was the strange black box—their two-way radio. The spirit women spoke to the box, and, amazingly, it spoke back to them. In ponderous discussions wise men arrived at a unanimous conclusion: Spirits came in all sizes. Hadn't they seen pictures of tiny "spirits" in Marilyn's Sears catalog? Little spirits, no larger than the joint of one's finger, were hiding inside the box, exchanging words with the visitors. Most likely, the men reasoned, these spirits lived under the graves of the burial mountain and came out at appointed times to speak from the box.

As twilight came Marilyn tuned her guitar. A cluster of onlookers observed every move. They halted their whispers at the sound of the music.

She strummed lightly for several moments, looking out at the people on the hillside, praying for them, for Judy, and for herself. Then, after a couple of introductory chords, she sang:

Jesus loves me, this I know,
For the Bible tells me so.
Little ones to him belong.
They are weak, but he is strong.

Long after the lights were out, Marilyn assessed her circumstances that were so different from life back home. Never before had she felt the weight of her responsibilities as she did now.

SIX

More Than Vowels and Consonants

*At last a boy looked up at her, his eyes bright with realization,
and said, "Omaka." Thrilled, Marilyn printed the word
phonetically in her notebook—her very first word in the Sepik
Iwam language!*

An alphabet was needed. The New Testament would never
be possible without an alphabet. Marilyn and Judy grabbed
their pens and notebooks and headed in separate directions
into the village.

Immediately each woman was surrounded by children,
excited to see what the "spirit women" would do. The children were at first hesitant to give out information.

Marilyn stepped up beside one of the support poles of a
house, patted it, then pointed up to the dwelling.

"House, house?" she said in English.

"Haus, haus," one boy repeated as he tried to pronounce
"house," holding a hand over his mouth to suppress his
embarrassment at the effort.

Still unsure about the new game, the children thronged
around her, watching her point at the house. At last a boy

looked up at her, his eyes bright with realization, and said, "*Omaka.*"

Thrilled, Marilyn printed the word phonetically in her notebook—her *very first* word in the Sepik Iwam language!

"O Lord," she exclaimed, "thank you! Here we go."

The people of Hauna had no concept of pencil, paper, or writing. When she held up her pencil, the children called it *tɨdiyɨn.* She later found it was their word for "thorn." They called her paper *yokwo:* "a banana leaf." They described her writing as *wɨni,* which meant "carving."

Each week the collection of words increased: *ipi* = "stool"; *i* = "canoe"; *mapuk* = "snake"; *kara* = "me"; *kɨra* = "you." Within just a few weeks the new linguists began forming a tentative alphabet by listing the sounds found in the words they had discovered. Sepik Iwam had several sounds that didn't occur in English.

The word *work* was *mɨi.*

The word *stomach* was *mhɨi,* which indicated to the linguists that the Sepik Iwam alphabet would have to include both a "voiced" *m* (as in English pronunciation) and a "voiceless" *m* (made by blowing air out the nose).

Sepik Iwam also had six vowel sounds, *a, e, i, o, u* and *ɨ.* Since the linguists didn't have a typewriter with that symbol, they typed an *i,* and then backspaced and placed a hyphen through it.

One day Marilyn pointed to a canoe and was told, "*i.*"

So she repeated the word, "*ii.*"

The children shook their heads in frustration. "*i!*"

She tried again, "*ii!*"

"No, no, no, what is wrong with your head?" they asked her. She couldn't understand those words, but she could read their tone of voice and body language.

Through this exchange Marilyn and Judy realized that

besides many voiceless consonants, Sepik Iwam also had lengthened vowels that would change a word's meaning by only sounding the vowel longer.

The word *i* is "canoe."

The word *ii* is "yesterday."

Hauna people were proud of their language. As Marilyn and Judy understood more, they never heard incorrect grammar during village conversations. They found the language beautiful and expressive and its grammar precise yet complicated. They learned that when speaking, they needed to indicate when the action took place. They couldn't simply speak of the past but had to clearly identify recent past, farther past, or long ago.

Walking through the village, Marilyn and Judy would often hear villagers calling out to them, *"Papi nami kira?"* Not yet knowing where the word breaks were, the linguists wrote down this string of sounds. Comparing notes, they surmised that this must be some kind of a greeting. But it couldn't be "good morning" because people called out *"Papi nami kira?"* to them in the evening also. However, when Marilyn and Judy would come up to a house and call out this sentence, everyone would look a bit confused and often smile in amusement.

After learning the various pronouns and a few more verbs, they were able to translate the phrase. The pronoun *you* was *kira*. The verb *nami* was "going." They then surmised that *papi* meant "where," a very difficult word to discover by itself. Besides adding a few more letters to the Sepik Iwam alphabet, this sentence gave them the clue as to what the word order should be for speaking a simple sentence.

Then came the glorious morning when, leaving the house, Marilyn met a young girl walking down the path. *"Papi nami kira?"* Marilyn asked. ("Where are you going?")

"*Kara numar nami,*" the girl responded pleasantly. ("I am going to the garden.")

Years before, Marilyn had exulted over hitting home runs, making field goals, and breaking the one hundred meter finish-line tape. All such emotions paled at the joy that came to her heart when, for the first time, she conversed in Sepik Iwam.

Judy, a skilled linguist, played a key role in seeking out vocabulary and sentence structure. While Marilyn gathered data from their neighbors, Judy excelled at organization. She frequently worked at her desk with Ogamar, an inquisitive man in his twenties, who became her faithful language helper. In the evenings, like excited stamp collectors comparing their discoveries, Marilyn and Judy sat in the lamplight and made a game of reviewing their expanding wealth of words and phrases.

They discovered thirty-two different ways to say "cut." For example, *niyar ati* is used when cutting down a tree. *Niyar tio* is used when cutting a tree into crosswise sections. And *niyar kaibi* is used when cutting a sago tree lengthwise.

As their conversation ability increased, due largely to Judy's work in describing Sepik Iwam sentence structure, the linguists began having basic but meaningful conversations with their neighbors. Many villagers, however, were still baffled by why it was taking the women so long to learn to speak Sepik Iwam properly.

Nokiyin, one of the oldest traditional healers, was said to be the "father of the whole village." He was keenly observant of what the newcomers were doing. Whenever possible, he shadowed their visits throughout the village. When he sensed that Marilyn finally had sufficient Sepik Iwam vocabulary to give him a clear answer to his nagging question, he asked, "Marilyn, what are you carving on that banana leaf with that thorn?"

"With this thorn I am carving your talk."

"My talk? You're carving the words that come out of my mouth?" he asked incredulously.

She assured him that was so.

The old man tapped her notebook, asking, "Well, what does that carving say?"

"It says, 'Kara omaka nami.'" ("I'm going to the house.")

"That's my talk!" he said as he rubbed the words with his fingers. "Yes, you've *carved* my talk!"

"Someday we want to teach your people how to carve it themselves," Marilyn told him. "Later we will put *Big Father Creator's Talk* on this banana leaf in your language, just as he spoke it."

From that day on Nokiyɨn helped in any way he could to aid the translators in learning his language.

After meditating on Marilyn and Judy's problem of pronunciation, Nokiyɨn made a suggestion to Headman Sauperi. Sauperi, too, was troubled to see them struggling, so he decided to take Nokiyɨn's suggestion. One day he assembled his people, inviting Judy and Marilyn. Mercifully, it was a long time before the women could reconstruct what he had said.

"As we all have seen from watching them, these two creatures are very weak," Sauperi began. "Many times we have watched them fall out of the canoe we gave them. Their feet slip when they try to climb up a notched pole into a house. Even our babies can speak our language, but these stupid creatures know only a few words. We have no understanding about why they are here. But they are friendly and very kind to our children, so we wish to help them. Why do they stammer when they try to speak our language? I think it is because of their food. How can anyone say our words without eating our food?"

As they agreed with their leader's logic, many looked in sympathy toward Marilyn and Judy.

So it was that the new translators complied with one of the underscored tenets of Wycliffe training: identify with the culture at every level feasible. In Hauna this would include sampling delicacies such as squirming, live termites and juicy, fat grubs, roasted shish-kebab style—medium rare!

Lord, Marilyn prayed silently, as she stared at the first offered rain-forest treat, *I'm willing to eat this all up if you will help me keep it all down!*

SEVEN

Fourteen Boys and a Shaman

That night as she indexed the day's findings, she burst into laughter. "Oh, Judy, look what I've been saying all afternoon! I certainly haven't made many friends today."

Childish squeals of laughter or squeals of fright accompanied Marilyn and Judy wherever they walked or paddled their canoe around Hauna.

"*Aiyo-oh! Aiyo-oh!* The ghosts are coming!" the children cried as they dove for cover behind their mothers' legs.

Within a few days after their arrival, Marilyn and Judy noticed that some of the children's curiosity was obviously stronger than their fear. Every daylight hour the new translators were inspected by inquisitive children, who studied the women's extraordinary habits of brushing their teeth and combing their unusual, straight hair. They were fascinated with the women's mirrors. Whatever the spiritlike beings did was fascinating, especially after it was determined that they were safe to be around.

In those earliest stages of their assignment, Judy and Marilyn learned that the Hauna people had preserved and perpetuated a large and intricate vocabulary. They could

47

specifically identify every tree, plant, bird, and insect that existed in their rain-forest kingdom.

This knowledge became even more evident one morning when Makapobiya and others invited Marilyn and Judy to walk into the jungle and learn the names of local trees. Following behind the talkative throng was like watching a National Geographic film, but live. Makapobiya and others gave enthusiastic responses to the linguists' requests for words, identifying every growing thing.

"Can you imagine someday publishing a Sepik Iwam textbook on botany?" Judy asked. "The research is all done."

"What a great dream. Let's do it!"

The major benefit from the jungle experience, however, came when some of the hunters noted the two women nursing arm scratches received when brushing past thorns. One man stepped up to Marilyn, smeared some of her blood on his finger, and tasted it.

Seated around the communal fire at the men's house that evening, a long discussion concluded that the pale-skinned women could not be spirits after all but were human beings, since everyone knew that spirits did not consist of flesh and blood.

Further breakthroughs in the villagers' acceptance resulted when Marilyn or Judy suffered from malarial fevers, infected sores, bleeding wounds, and even cried like people; spirits don't do these things. As Hauna finally began to accept these pale creatures as human like themselves, the children started calling them *Apu* (Mama).

Running the paths of Hauna was a "gang" of little boys, ranging in age from five to nine. Since they had fewer chores than the older children, they used their free time to watch the women. Usually these boys arrived at the door even before the women had dressed and eaten breakfast.

The boys were always eager to see what crazy things these women would do next. At first they refused the invitation to come into the newcomers' house, but they loved to press their faces against the screen door and watch every movement inside. Whenever Marilyn or Judy would walk close to the door, the young observers would dash away so fast that they often became a tangle of arms and legs as they tumbled down the stairs. The women provided a great deal of amusement, especially when they showed themselves uncoordinated in a canoe or inept at starting a fire.

Marilyn and Judy enjoyed the boys' antics too. Once when Hyombwan and Wikmwo were engrossed in studying the photos in a *National Geographic* magazine, they suddenly yelled, threw the book down, and raced out of the house. They had flipped to a page picturing a huge snake, and since they had never before seen something that wasn't real, they were convinced that the photo was an actual snake.

Once they conquered their fear, the boys never refused any food that was offered to them. It wasn't that they were underfed by their families, but they were convinced that if they ate the women's food, their tongues would be loosened to speak English.

The boys also appeared committed to drilling the Sepik Iwam language into the women's heads, one word and phrase at a time. Marilyn and Judy became convinced that no translators anywhere had ever had language teachers any more dedicated than this group of Hauna boys. They never seemed to tire, coming day after day to watch and teach.

Equally as fascinated and committed was the old shaman, Nokiyin. His smiling face and pleasant, courteous disposition made him a desired friend.

Puzzled by their desire to live in his village, Nokiyin observed the unusual actions and words of these peculiar women. He happened along one day when Marilyn was out on her daily rounds of vocabulary gathering, using her *Translator's Field Guide*. Wycliffe linguists valued this book for its lists of necessary introductory vocabulary to elicit when learning an unwritten language.

This day, in an effort to find the word for "jump," she was jumping up and down. Laughing heartily, the swarm of children joined in jumping alongside her, thinking the action to be some new game.

Sitting on a log nearby, Nokiyin stared at her. Shaking his head, he finally blurted out, *"Kirawaowainanai!"*

Thinking he might have just given the answer to her vocabulary search, Marilyn hurried over to him. "Please say that again." He repeated his comment over and over until she had written it phonetically.

Kirawaowainanai. That's an awfully long word for the verb jump, she thought. Next to this new entry in her notebook, she recorded that this long word might be the verb *jump*, or perhaps a sentence containing the verb *to jump*.

For the rest of the afternoon she visited her village neighbors, trying out her new sentence, thinking she was saying something similar to "I am jumping." She was met with puzzled expressions and laughter.

That night as she indexed the day's findings, she burst into laughter.

"Oh, Judy, look what I've been saying all afternoon! I certainly haven't made many friends today. He didn't give me the word for 'jump.'"

By cross-checking previous tentative vocabulary, she concluded that the translation of Nokiyɨn's remark was: "Why are you acting so stupid?"

"Whanabinao—my name is Whanabinao."
As Marilyn tried to repeat the name correctly, as well as write it phonetically in her notebook, the boys sitting in front of her burst into laughter and teased her about her incorrect pronunciation.
"What are you laughing about this morning?" Nokiyɨn asked the boys.
"Just listen to *Apu* when she tries to say my name," Whanabinao explained amid the gales of laughter.
"Or my name," Mirinuwau added, "Or Hyombwan or Wikmwo's name."
"Why do you think it is so hard for her to pronounce some of our names?" Adiyawai asked Nokiyɨn.
"She must not be eating enough sago."
It was one thing to have discovered that most Sepik Iwam consonants also had voiceless counterparts and to be aware of the "ɨ" vowel—but another thing to train the tongue to reproduce all the sounds correctly.
Nokiyɨn remained curious about Marilyn's writing in her ever present notebook. He became especially helpful in relating vocabulary to the Sepik Iwam culture. Marilyn could ask him many things relating to Hauna village lifestyle. All the probing questions she had quizzed him on so far he had gladly answered. But dare she be so bold as to ask him *that* question? One day when the boys were absent, she couldn't hold it in any longer.
"Nokiyɨn, why do you men wear only a vine around your waist?"

51

Grinning, but with the affronted air of a Victorian gentleman, he retorted, "You don't expect us to run around naked, do you?"

Marilyn had begun to receive used clothing from folks back home. Offering garments as a corrective to nudity would have been pointless and highly insulting, but having clothes to ward off the hot sun and biting insects was another matter. Some of Hauna's citizens gratefully began wearing dresses, shirts, and trousers.

One shipment from Valparaiso included a pair of trousers with a green belt. At first glance it looked like a sure fit for Nokiyin. He received the gift with evident gratitude late one afternoon and paddled quickly across the river. Walking up to his house, he called out excitedly, "Look! Look what the two *misses* have given me!"

At dawn the next day he was back at the base of the translators' house, exclaiming, "Marilyn! Judy! I'm here, and I'm all dressed up in my new clothes!"

"Come on up, we're ready to start work."

He proudly bounced across the bark floor, shoulders back and obviously thrilled with his new apparel.

He had left the trousers at home and was clad only in the green belt!

"Marilyn, look at me!" Nokiyin said one day. "I'm an old man, and my skin is wrinkled; my eyes are poor; my fingers have arthritis." He rubbed his brown wrinkled neck and chest with a gnarled hand. "I've been watching you as you walk through our village with your banana leaf, carving my talk."

He paused and leaned forward. "My father and many of my relatives died many years ago. They knew nothing about God. And for me, it's too late! I'm too old to read my own talk." Looking intently into her eyes, he asked, "Did you know a long time ago, when you were a little girl, that there were people here in Papua New Guinea like me?"

"Yes, I read books," she answered. "I knew about Papua New Guinea."

"Then, Marilyn, why did it take you so long to come?"

Marilyn drew in a breath to give an answer, but she had none. She felt broken. Inwardly she cried, *Lord, O Lord, please don't let others wait like this man had to wait.*

When their grasp of the language increased and they had settled on the alphabet and had the basics of the grammatical structure, Marilyn and Judy began testing their language analysis by trying to teach Sepik Iwam speakers to read.

As Marilyn and the boys were writing out a rough draft for a new primer, the boys would mimic the sound represented by the letters. One day Marilyn noticed that Kariman and Yaumor were holding their booklets upside down. When she turned them the right way, the boys couldn't seem to read without tilting their heads. She soon realized that they had been seated across the table during the early lessons and had begun to learn to recognize the letters the way they had first seen them—upside down!

Besides the fourteen boys, the early reading classes began with several interested adults: Ogamar and Yaka, who were Judy and Marilyn's adult language helpers, plus others. The linguists needed to test how well a Sepik Iwam speaker could understand the trial alphabet and grammatical structure. Since the boys caught on more quickly than the adults, they became the first Sepik Iwam literacy teachers and were the first Christians. Eventually they were the main translators.

Marilyn remembered her little red grammar school reader:

> *See Dick run.*
> *See Jane run.*
> *Run, run, run.*

Obviously, Hauna children didn't know anything about Dick and Jane. Working with Yaka and Nokiyin, primers were written using stories to fit Sepik Iwam culture:

> *See the cassowary bird.*
> *See the long python.*
> *See the big crocodile.*
> *Run! Run! Run!*

Yapawi, a teenage uncle to most of the boys who filled Marilyn and Judy's house, had spent a short time away from Hauna during the first few years the women lived there. While Yapawi attended a mission school 250 miles away, he changed his name to Joel. He said he had become a Christian, but it wasn't until he heard the gospel in his heart language—Sepik Iwam—that he truly comprehended what it meant to be a Christian. Since he was a bit older, he became the natural leader of the young men.

Throughout the next few years, the fourteen boys all followed a common New Guinea practice of changing their names. They didn't like their village names being mispronounced and misspelled by the periodically visiting government officers, so they enjoyed flipping through the Melanesian Pidgin Bible to pick out new names.

"Here we go, learning your names all over again," Marilyn teased the boys, "but at least this time I can spell and pronounce them."

"We have a new name for you, too," Kwarin (now Paul) informed her.

"Oh no, what is it?"

"Gecko! We like to call you the Gecko because you're always dashing around like a little lizard, supervising four or five projects at the same time!"

"They're melting the ice! They're melting the ice!" This woeful announcement rippled around the village. Whenever Marilyn and Judy defrosted their kerosene refrigerator, everyone knew they were going away on a long trip. But this time they weren't just going to Ukarumpa. Marilyn and Judy needed a furlough; they were going back to America.

Weakened physically by repeated bouts of malaria and by long periods of oppressive heat, both were ready for their first furlough. It had been five years since they had seen their families and partners back home.

The morning of their departure dawned with loud wailing. Their house was surrounded by villagers, and it was almost impossible to reach their canoe. Everyone was wailing, wanting one last touch or rub of their skin because they didn't know if they would ever see them again.

Just before the women stepped into the canoe to leave, Nokiyin, Makapobiya, Sauperi, and other older villagers came up to them. "Look at my face," they each said. "You need to remember my face. Look at my face. I'm an old man. I won't be here when you return."

"Who will help us with our sores?"

"Our throats are worried about the school."

"Don't let your throats worry. We'll be back."

"What about Papa God's carving? You have The Big Book and we only have a little bit of it."

"We'll be back."

Wailing from the village rang in their ears for miles as they headed downriver.

Reverse culture shock was a new experience. After five years away from the U.S., Marilyn collided with the fast-paced lifestyle, new fashions, and changed relationships. She felt like a foreigner in her own country. However, she felt welcomed at churches and discovered scattered pockets of concerned and committed Christians who believed in missions as passionately as she did. Praying and providing for missions enhanced their lives as much as active duty enriched her own.

"God has sent me to a people who have a morality and an ethical code that would put many Christians to shame," Marilyn told one congregation. "Happiness characterizes their lives. They are incredibly unselfish in the way they share and care. Yet they have animistic beliefs, so they live in fear. They believe implicitly in a spirit world. Despite their smiling facades, they are often tormented by anxiety and uncertainty. They need God's Word in their own language so they can know about Jesus' love and peace."

A highlight of this U.S. visit was spending time with Wycliffe's founder, Cameron Townsend, and his wife, Elaine. Marilyn was challenged all over again by these

dynamic and successful Christian leaders. "Uncle Cam"
became a major influence in her life during the next few
years.

Hauna turned out en masse a year later to greet Marilyn
and Judy as they arrived by canoe from Ambunti. Everyone
stroked their arms or faces in greeting.

"You can go into your house," Joel said, "but with careful
steps."

Marilyn glanced up toward their house and saw that it
was sagging and badly in need of replacement. In that same
moment she saw a pile of construction materials that had
been floated in during high-water season. She and Judy felt
cared for by the anticipation of this need.

It took half an hour before excitement subsided. Even
then, many people remained as the women entered their
rickety residence. Sun-baked and sweaty from the day-long
ride in the canoe, Marilyn was thrilled to find the old
improvised shower stall intact and lovingly supplied with
freshly drawn buckets of river water. The water was warm
and delightfully refreshing.

"Lord," Marilyn whispered during her shower, "thank you
for these dear friends."

At the height of her euphoria, a young python dropped
from the roof thatch overhead. Screaming, she pressed herself against the curtain. With the house full of people, she
couldn't escape to another room! The python lingered a
moment at her feet, then slithered away.

"So much for my welcome back," she exhaled.

EIGHT

Thorn Cures

*The wide-eyed spitters—and much of the village—
moved in closely. What on earth, they wondered, did bending
thorns against an old man's buttocks have to do with driving a
spirit of sickness from his head and chest?*

Since adult brothers and their families lived together in one
big house, as many as four traditional doctors lived in each
Sepik Iwam residence. Their primary responsibility was the
physical welfare of those under whose roof they lived. Spitters, as they were called, were never criticized. They applied
their traditional therapies, many of them effective, while
they also sought the presence and possession of the spirits.
If a sufferer died, it was the will of the spirits, not the failure
of incantations or traditional remedies. Consequently,
people took slowly to Marilyn's tackle box/medical kit.

Marilyn had never once considered a career in health care.
Yet, as the villagers' confidence in her grew, people came
with their cuts and bruises, aches and pains. But if an illness
reached such severity that a jungle doctor became involved,
neither Marilyn nor Judy were allowed to offer assistance.

Meanwhile, deaths and burials were frequent. Marilyn's
heart ached to think of the many who might have been

spared by a course of tablets and injections. Pneumonia killed about as many as malaria did. Yaws—similar to leprosy—elephantiasis, hepatitis, tuberculosis, and a myriad of terminal infections took lives every month. The prevalence of sickness and death was overwhelming.

Out of their growing affection for Marilyn and Judy, people accepted aspirin, antimalarial medicine, and diarrhea tablets but promptly spat them out the moment the women turned their backs. Small adhesive bandages, on the other hand, became an instant hit—both as a treatment and a decorative adornment. But when it came to the tackle box's ominous thorns, the injection needles, the vote was unanimously negative: "*Ningiga!*"

One afternoon Marilyn visited the home of Nokiyin, her friend and consultant, who lay critically ill with malaria and pneumonia, a combination that was usually a death sentence. Would the traditional healers consider him an exception and permit her to administer an injection? She immediately fetched her tackle box.

"*Ningiga!*" snapped the resident spitter when she showed him a loaded syringe.

Marilyn's frustration and sorrow left her numb.

Lord, O Lord, please let me get a chance to give Nokiyin a shot.

Early the next morning Marilyn awakened to soft wailing in the distance. *How is Nokiyin?* she wondered.

"Marilyn!" she heard outside her house. "We've brought an old man; he's very sick. You come down here and shoot him."

Excited, Marilyn grabbed the medical box, prepared two injections, one an antimalarial treatment and the other penicillin, and headed down the stairs. When she saw they were holding Nokiyin up against a pole, she knew the spitters didn't expect him to live, so they were using him as a test case. She didn't care about their motives. She was relieved to finally have the opportunity to save his life.

"Nokiyin has terrible pain in his head," one spitter informed her. "His chest and ribs are in pain, too."

"I have medicine for all those problems," Marilyn assured him and the forming crowd.

Since Nokiyin was wearing only his vine, he was all ready for his first shot. Thanking God and praying for guidance in the same breath, Marilyn wiped an alcohol gauze across his leathery buttocks and poised the needle for injection. She gave the men a quick glance and a nervous smile. Hesitating for only a moment, she moved forward with the speed of a striking serpent.

Ping!

The needle bent! She might as easily have tried to inoculate one of the tough, cured crocodile hides!

"Please, Lord, help!" she implored aloud.

Acting as if bending the needle were standard procedure, she replaced the bent thorn. The wide-eyed spitters—and much of the village—moved in closely. What on earth, they wondered, did bending thorns against an old man's buttocks have to do with driving a spirit of sickness from his head and chest?

Trembling now, Marilyn attached her second, and last, needle. She selected what felt like a softer area of skin, disinfected it, then jabbed the syringe as hard as she could. With success! She took a satisfied step back.

"Nokiyin isn't sick at his bottom!" one of the men scolded angrily.

"He needed medicine for his head, his chest, and his ribs! Now you've wasted all the medicine in the place where he isn't sick," spat out another.

As they carried the limp Nokiyɨn back to his house to die, one muttered, "I don't know about you people, but we're never sick down there."

As the sun set that evening, and as hundreds of awed villagers looked on, Nokiyɨn began talking and eating. He even walked through the village as if he'd never been ill! Marilyn didn't know a great deal about medicine, but she knew that the little amount of medicine she'd given Nokiyɨn wasn't enough to produce this miracle of recovery. God had intervened in his life and in her ministry to Hauna village.

"Papa God didn't want me to die," Nokiyɨn told her that evening. "Papa God wants me to see his Talk carved on the banana leaves."

After the breakthrough with Nokiyɨn's miraculous recovery, Marilyn and Judy were barraged with calls to do medical work. The medicine they had brought with them performed what the Sepik Iwam people viewed as astounding acts of magic.

Previously, the only treatments for physical ailments were performed by the shamans. In Hauna alone there were about 160 of these practitioners, mostly men. Some, like Headman Sauperi, were the leaders of their clans and were highly respected for their powers and ability to summon spirits.

For the more common ailments, the shamans had their own traditional cures. A certain leaf, when chewed, treated diarrhea efficiently. The skins and meat of the papaya fruit and heated banana leaves were used effectively for treating certain infections. Pain due to arthritis or injury could be eased by the nettles leaf. These plants were grown close to the houses so they were handy when needed.

No matter how exotic such practices seemed to Marilyn
and Judy, they sought to win the friendship of the traditional healers, discussing modes of treatment and observing
their traditional techniques. However, when they progressed
from the traditional medicines to summoning the spirits,
Marilyn and Judy parted company from them.

"Marilyn, Judy, wake up!" Joel called out. "I need one of
you to come with me to Inasi's house. His daughter is
dying."

Trying not to slip with the tackle box in hand, Marilyn
hurried in the darkness. She had heard the wailing for hours
now.

When she entered the house, she could hardly breathe.
Smoke permeated all village dwellings. The Sepik Iwam
people cherished their fires, if for no other reason than to
keep mosquitoes at bay. Unknown to them, the smoke also
increased their susceptibility to lung infection. When someone was ill, a dwelling would be even more filled with
smoke because the openings to the outdoors would have
been boarded up to hold back invading spirits.

Inasi and his wife, Mary, were kneeling beside their desperately ill daughter, putting their heads on her sick body,
caressing her face, feeling her arms, touching her eyes and
lips. Everyone was wailing, with the parental outcry sounding like a baleful duet above the discordant chorus. Marilyn
had rarely seen any parents more loving to their children.

Since a traditional spitter was already beside the child,
Marilyn knew that she would not be allowed to offer any
medicine this night.

The shaman was waving a small branch and chewing gingerroot. He was spitting constantly, not in a vulgar way but

with ritualistic precision and genuine compassion. Marilyn watched in horror as he cut tiny slits in the child's chest, then spat gingerroot juice into the bleeding cuts.

The wailing intensified, rising and falling rhythmically. The spitter began to chant while he continued to chew on the gingerroot. Calling out for the avenging spirit to possess him, Marilyn saw first one of his legs and then the other begin to shake. Before long his whole body began to tremble. She jumped when the shaman cried out, now totally possessed by the spirit.

"What is happening to that shaman?" Marilyn whispered when she could finally catch her breath.

"A spirit is now controlling him."

The shaman then lurched around the room while he spoke in another language. From what Marilyn had been told, she knew a traditional healer would not be this frantic if he didn't think his patient was close to death.

Eventually he arched back and moaned, *"Saeya bɨdi yao! Saeya haingikaika!"* It was the shaman's pronouncement of death. ("She has died. Plant her!")

One day a twelve-year-old girl was brought to them with a seriously infected toe. By the horrible smell, they knew it was gangrene. Nervously, Marilyn put in an emergency call to Ukarumpa to a medical advisor.

"The toe will have to be cut off," she was told. "You'll have to do it quickly. Time is of the essence. She will die before you can get her out to a hospital."

"But, Doc," Marilyn objected, fighting off a wave of nausea, "I know nothing about surgery! I've never cut off anything more serious than a hangnail."

"It's the only way," the doctor replied. "First, get a disinfected razor blade. Sterilize the wound, then tell me when you're ready and do exactly what I tell you."

"Oh, Judy, I can't! You've got to do it!"

Trembling, Marilyn wrapped her arms around the girl and buried her face next to the girl's while Judy skillfully performed the operation, following the doctor's instructions. In a short time the surgery and cleanup was done. Within a few days the wound would be healing well, and the patient, minus a toe, would continue to lead an active life.

That evening as the two "surgeons" started to prepare their supper, Marilyn picked up the can they had set out that morning. "Oh no! Judy, I can't eat hot dogs tonight!"

In fact, it took many months before Marilyn could even look at a hot dog again!

The year after their furlough, after much prayer and discussion, Judy left Marilyn to return to Ukarumpa for another assignment.

Marilyn was devastated. She couldn't imagine continuing alone, but she also couldn't imagine leaving Hauna. She did sense God's comforting assurance that he would continue to be with her, however. Administrators at Ukarumpa routed numerous visitors and short-term partners to assist her. Hauna became a favorite Shangri-la for her vacationing friends from Ukarumpa, so she was seldom alone for any extended time.

She had formed reliable friendships among the Sepik Iwam people, so even during those weeks when she was alone, she felt no apprehension. However, at times, loneliness crushed in on her, which prompted prayers and dreams for a new teammate. In God's timing it was six years before anyone joined her full-time.

NINE

Crocodiles and Calculators

"This is very bad," she complained to Sauperi. "Those traders are cheating your people who work so hard killing crocodiles."

One day Marilyn came upon Sauperi puffing on a home-made cigarette and was startled to see that the smoldering tobacco paper was actually an Australian twenty-dollar bill. Several years earlier he had worked on a plantation, and he still treasured the coins he had earned but obviously deemed the paper money valuable only as cigarette paper. Coins, made with holes through their shiny metal centers, were threaded onto vine segments and worn around the neck as decoration.

"Oh, Big Father," Marilyn exclaimed. "May I show you something?"

He handed her his burning cigarette, and she pointed to the printing on the paper currency. "This is Australian carving," she told him. "The Head Man in Australia tells you this paper will buy more rice than the coins around your neck."

Sauperi laughed heartily, thinking Marilyn had told him a joke. When he saw that she was serious, he retrieved the cigarette, returned it to his mouth and waved his hand, excusing himself.

A few days later traders arrived in their routine search for crocodile skins. Marilyn watched aghast as she saw Hauna men exchange skins, worth several hundred dollars or more, for a few fishhooks, a small bag of salt, flashlights, or a handful of coins.

"This is very bad," she complained to Sauperi. "Those traders are cheating your people who work so hard killing crocodiles. Remember what I told you about the Australian paper money? I told you the truth."

Sauperi looked at Marilyn in minimal belief. Always desiring to improve the lot of his people, he glanced at the traders, then back to Marilyn. He gave a gesture of frustration.

Something clicked in Marilyn's thinking. The Sepik Iwam people did not have numbers beyond twenty, the sum of their fingers and toes. Teaching them the value of money might provide a breakthrough toward teaching them to read.

On her next trip to Wewak, a coastal town, she purchased two dozen calculators and as many measuring tapes. She also secured government lists on the value of marketable rain-forest items, such as crocodile skins.

The morning after returning to Hauna, she asked Paul to summon several crocodile hunters to her house. These brave men went out on moonless nights and, gliding their canoes across silent waters, held flaming torches above their heads. The flames reflected in the eyes of the crocodiles, submerged except for the vulnerable brow. Once a crocodile was temporarily blinded by the torch's light, the hunter would send a lethal spear deep into the reptile's head, careful not to destroy the skin.

Marilyn placed the calculators and measuring tapes on the table. To these she added a string of coins together with examples of "worthless" Australian paper money. Picking up a currency sample and holding it alongside the string of coins, she said, "This government banana leaf will buy three 55-pound bags of rice." Lifting the coins, she added, "These money pieces will only buy one 22-pound bag."

Eyes widened and silence engulfed the room. Marilyn's pulse quickened. Makapobiya had provided a well-seasoned crocodile skin for her demonstration. Draping it across both arms, the excited teacher asked, "How many small bags of salt will you give for this skin?"

"Two bags," one man said.

Another stepped up to Marilyn, examined the pelt like a seasoned entrepreneur, and said, "It is old. It was not well salted. I give one bag for this skin and six boar tusks."

An argument erupted into a cacophony of voices.

"Quiet, please!" Marilyn called out. The men complied.

She now held up the government price list and said, "This banana leaf was carved by the government to help you sell crocodile skins. You have been badly cheated and given dishonest payment for valuable skins." She held out the price list and, with a tinge of sorrow in her voice, added, "Since you cannot count further than your toes and fingers, and since you cannot read, you have no way to protect yourselves."

Using the blackboard, she began teaching basic arithmetic.

For several months, more than twenty men gathered nightly by the light of Marilyn's kerosene lantern for math lessons. Eventually she introduced a calculator, making numbers appear and change and disappear. The class gathered closely to observe this wonder that had come to Hauna village.

"You need never again be cheated by the crocodile-skin buyers."

Next she demonstrated how to determine a skin's worth as specified on the government price lists. She showed them how to use a carpenter's tape measure, which to their delight used the same numbers as they had learned on their calculators. Instead of merely fishhooks and salt bags, the men now saw they could earn large amounts of spendable cash while staying in their own village. Marilyn offered to help increase the variety of goods in the Hauna store, at prices guaranteed to be no more than what one would pay in Wewak, New Guinea's northwestern seaport.

Whoops of delight echoed out onto the night air.

One, two, three, today—a, b, c, tomorrow! Marilyn thought.

As the Hauna men waited for the next traders to visit, skins were carefully cured, and the experts helped to train those less adept.

One day the crocodile traders' canoe entered the village. The drums beat out the announcement of their arrival, and men headed to the riverbank to lay out their skins. From the vantage point of her house on the hill, Marilyn and Paul looked down at the scene. They could hear the dialogue going on.

"Well, for this skin," the trader said in Melanesian Pidgin, "I'll give you two bags of salt." Without bothering to measure the skin he continued, "For this one I'll give you two batteries."

"Paul," Marilyn said, "I think it's time for you to go down now." This was the day the men had studied for, and they were ready.

Armed with a tape measure, a calculator, and the government price list for skins, Paul cordially addressed one of the traders. "Excuse me, Masta. What you are doing to my people is not right."

"You shut your mouth! You are nothing more than a jungle boy!" the trader shot back. "What do you know?!"

Showing respect and natural politeness, Paul said again, "Excuse me, Masta. I would like to show you."

Pulling out the tape measure, he laid it against the skin, then wrote down the numbers. After checking the government price list for a skin of that dimension, he softly said, "This skin is worth 300 pounds."

The Hauna men were not cheated by crocodile-skin traders that day!

This episode sent positive shock waves throughout the village. Marilyn's literacy work finally had the attention of the adults. She also received increased respect from Sauperi. Inspired by the calculator phenomenon, a handful of adults and scores of youth came to the classroom located underneath her house.

TEN

Airmail

Marilyn looked at the leaflet and asked,
"What is carved on this banana leaf?"

"How can we know?"

"The carvings are words from your language."

Sauperi looked in silent marvel at the little handbill.

"Sauperi, I need to go to Ukarumpa for a month. Would you like me to bring something back to you from the store?"

"My wife needs a new shovel for the garden, and I need a new ax. I also need some new fishing line and hooks."

General interest in learning to read and write their own language was neither constant nor spreading rapidly among the people of Hauna. Marilyn prayed that her next trip to Ukarumpa for a literacy seminar would give her some new ideas for sparking their interest.

One evening at Ukarumpa, as she was going over the shopping list to make sure she had bought everything she needed before returning to the village, a creative idea popped into her mind. She wrote Hauna village a letter, informing them of additional items she had found available at Ukarumpa's store. In the letter she listed the new products and asked, "Do you want me to get these items, too? If so, let me know your shopping list via a letter."

Hauna people loved watching the flying canoes. If they happened to be in the jungle when one was in the area, they would climb a tree to watch it. Flying canoes were only seen high in the sky, higher than the birds flew, often even higher than the clouds. Except for the few times the pontoon plane landed on the river, airplanes never flew low over Hauna. What if one did, Marilyn wondered, and dropped many copies of her letter to Hauna, written in the Sepik Iwam language?

The aviation department at Ukarumpa approved her idea. Before Marilyn's return to Hauna, one of SIL's planes flew at treetop altitude over the village, dropping several hundred banana leaves with the printed message. As the papers fluttered to the ground, some people were terrified. Children screamed, some in fear, some in delight. Nothing in ancestral lore told of anything so exciting. As the plane droned back toward the mountains, the villagers began scrambling to collect the leaflets on the ground and those floating on the river.

A few of the students that met nightly under Marilyn's house understood some of the words—but not enough to understand the message.

"*Apu!*" Sauperi used the name most were now calling Marilyn.

Her motorized canoe had just returned from the airstrip at Ambunti. The village leader joined the throng who came to greet her as she returned from her month at Ukarumpa.

"It is sad you went away," he began. "A flying canoe

passed over our heads three sunrises ago, moving through the air as low as the birds when they go from tree to tree." He held out one of the leaflets for his friend to see. "As many as there are fingers and toes in all Hauna, these fell from the canoe's belly."

Marilyn looked at the leaflet and asked, "What is carved on this banana leaf?"

"How can we know?"

"The carvings are words from your language," Marilyn told him.

Sauperi looked in silent marvel at the little handbill. "Tell the words to me, Marilyn."

"This banana leaf carving tells you about some new products I saw in the Ukarumpa store. I could have brought them back with me," Marilyn explained. "Pots and pans, metal coffee cups, fabric for clothing, mirrors, razor blades . . ."

"For our village store!" the headman interrupted. "You could have brought new things for us if we had told you?"

"That's right. If you could have read this and sent me a message, I could have brought these extra things back for the Hauna store."

"But, Marilyn, you know we can't read."

"You can't read your own language? You have one of the most beautiful and important languages. Yet you and your wise leaders and your people cannot read what you speak. I am an outsider, but am I the only one who can read your language?"

The next morning Sauperi called a meeting of the village. The men had been planning a boar hunt, so the people understood that this meeting must be important.

"Only Marilyn can read the banana leaf carvings of our language," Sauperi began. He held up one of the leaflets that everyone recognized. "Some of you have feared she was stealing our words, but now I see this is not true. This proves that she does not steal our talk. Instead, she has come to live with us to teach us how to read and write our own language."

"But what about her black box?" a man argued, referring to the tape recorder she often used in search of vocabulary. "Her black box eats our words. She could fill the box with all our stories and sayings and take the box to her country. Then we would be left with the mouths of dead men."

"It is true the box eats our words, but it spits the words back out again," Makapobiya said to support Sauperi's explanation. "The black box is the way she brings the sound of our words close to her ears. This is how she learns to speak with the sounds we use when we talk."

Sauperi silenced the argument. "Our people must learn to understand the carving on the banana leaf," he said, rattling the leaflet for emphasis.

Little did they know how "life-and-death" important letter writing would one day be.

Sauperi announced that all could attend the village school. In addition, he assigned a number of the brightest younger men to become students. Among them were Danny, Paul, Matthew, Hosea, Ogamar, Joel, Gideon, Jonah, and a half dozen others. From this group would come future teachers and leaders as well as, in answer to years of prayer, the translation team!

Nightly for two hours, depending on the mosquitoes, Sepik Iwam academics met beneath Marilyn's house. Students collected discarded canoes to serve as benches. Marilyn cut plywood into small pieces and coated them with chalkboard paint. On a large blackboard she wrote words for students to learn.

Old and young now arrived for evening classes. Kerosene

lanterns, scarcely brighter than the moonlight, provided illumination. Enthusiastic men, women, and teenagers started down the road to literacy.

Despite another bout of malaria that sapped her energy and numbed her appetite, Marilyn dragged herself down to the classroom night after night, even while taking the treatment medicine. Hosea, a faithful handyman, lit the gas lanterns and prepared for the students who came.

She could see the light at the end of the tunnel. She was ecstatic, but she was also weary to the bone.

ELEVEN

Trichinosis for Jesus

*High-water season brought not only boar hunting time but
also a mysterious sickness that took many lives each year.
Agonizing pain accompanied this ailment. It was
devastating to watch six tormented deaths that next week.*

Hauna bristled with excitement one morning as the men
prepared a foray into the rain forest to hunt wild boar. They
returned by nightfall with an abundance of meat.

Marilyn was already tucked under her mosquito net when
she heard from across the river, "Marilyn! I've killed a wild
boar. Come and eat with me."

Headman Sauperi was inviting Marilyn to a feast at his
residence. His request was not to be ignored, so even
though it was dark and about eight o'clock, she crawled out
from under her mosquito net, splashed on some repellent,
and paddled her canoe across to Sauperi's house.

The main course was roasted wild boar. Sauperi reached
into the fire with some bamboo tongs and grabbed a prime
chunk, slapping it on a leaf before handing it to her. As she
started to eat it, she could feel the stiff boar hairs between
her fingers.

She couldn't help thinking that if she had to eat it, it was a good thing the light was dim, the room's only illumination coming from the fire pit. As she bit into the meat, she found it was so tough she had to work hard to tear off a piece to chew. Despite the faint light, she could see that the meat farther away from the skin was still quite red.

"Tomorrow I'm coming to your house. I want another cup of coffee and one of those sweet biscuits," Sauperi said conversationally.

"I can rub some more arthritis oil into your shoulders, too," Marilyn said, talking around a wad of rubbery meat.

It was an important invitation and meal to be shared with the headman and his wife, Usu, and another opportunity to talk to them about Jesus.

After politely eating all the meat but leaving the hairy skin, she headed back to bed.

High-water season brought not only boar hunting time but also a mysterious sickness that took many lives each year. Agonizing pain accompanied this ailment. It was devastating to watch six tormented deaths that next week. Marilyn talked to the doctor at Ukarumpa, but none of the treatments he suggested seemed to stop the misery and dying.

Then it attacked her. Deathly ill, she called Ukarumpa on the radio for a plane to come to Ambunti. A bed was made for her in the motorized canoe. With Paul at the rudder, she made the miserable, pain-racked 110-mile trip downriver to Ambunti. The next day an SIL plane flew her to Ukarumpa.

"I'm sorry," the doctor at Ukarumpa told her, "but your condition is beyond our diagnostic capabilities. You must fly back to the States as soon as possible."

After baffling experts in five different hospitals in the U.S., the gravely ill translator entered a diagnostic clinic in Chicago, where several specialists became intently interested in her condition.

"You work in New Guinea?" the senior among them asked.

"In the jungles," Marilyn replied weakly.

"Eat any unusual foods?"

Marilyn pictured food gifts from her Hauna neighbors and said, "Y-yes, sometimes."

"Such as?"

"Well, things like, uh, like termites, grubs, wild boar. . . ."

"How well is it cooked," the specialist broke in, "this wild boar meat?"

"Rare."

"It's amazing you're still alive!" they told her the next day when the diagnosis was concluded. "Your body is full of parasites. Due to eating that poorly cooked wild boar meat, you have a critical case of trichinosis." The specialist paused, looking down at his patient like a caring father. "Besides that, you have hepatitis, a severe ear fungus, malaria, hypoglycemia, and a suspicious spot on one of your lungs."

Marilyn managed a brief smile and quipped, "No wonder I haven't been feeling very well!" Then she asked seriously, "But why did *I* live when so many in the village died?"

"You probably had a more balanced diet, to begin with. But you're not out of the woods yet; you still have a long way to go. There is no cure for trichinosis. It's a matter of time. The worms will slowly become entombed in your muscle tissue."

Jokingly the doctor added, "Just don't let anyone take a bite of out you."

Her recovery took over a year.

During her beginning literacy classes in Hauna, she had taught Paul and a few others the basics of writing and receiving letters. So as soon as she could hold a pen, she wrote to Paul:

> *The doctors in America have explained why so many of your people die during pig-hunting season. It is the way you cook your meat. Tell everyone that they must cook it long enough and hot enough until there is no more redness.*

Since the day that letter arrived in Hauna village in 1974, no one has died of the lethal disease. Because of that, Marilyn considered it a privilege to have trichinosis for Jesus!

Trichinosis was only one battle won.

Although Marilyn usually held her peace, her temper, when aroused, could scorch the atmosphere. The people got a taste of that temper at a village meeting. During one of the devastating pneumonia epidemics that periodically swept through the village, people assembled to mourn the dead and to discuss methods of saving the sick.

Among the crowd were the fourteen boys, who were now literacy teachers, even though they were only young teens. Standing off to one side, Marilyn listened in mounting anger as the elders finally agreed that only the shamans would be allowed to treat the sick and to determine what might be causing the spirits to bring such disaster to the village.

Catching sight of Marilyn, the presiding elder called out: "*Apu* Marilyn, do you have anything to say?"

"Do I!" she shot back. Straightening to her full five-feet-two-inches height, she strode to the center of the gathering. "I wonder what I'm doing here! I came to Hauna as a friend— a friend who has brought not only strong medicine but a strong Spirit from the Big Father Creator, the Holy Spirit. The medicine I've brought, if used in time, could save many of your people from a feverish death. But now you give me no opportunity to use this strong medicine or to ask the Holy Spirit of the Big Father for healing. I may just as well pack up and go home!"

On and on she went. In trying to teach the leaders about the physical causes of illnesses, she realized that explaining germs was difficult enough in English, let alone in a language she didn't fully know. They asked, "Who is this germ? Where does he live?"

Then one of the young literacy teachers, Gideon, stepped forward and said, "You don't want to use modern medicine because you are nothing but bush people!"

Stung by this name-calling, the crowd set up a chilling yell, surging toward the teachers and their supporters with menacing clubs and canoe paddles. In the middle of the skirmish, pushed and shoved from all sides, Marilyn thought, *My time has come.* Before long, nearly a hundred joined the fight, taking sides, with many not really knowing what they were fighting about. Gideon pulled her through the mob, got her into a canoe, and paddled her to safety across the river.

"Well, so much for this day," Marilyn sighed.

By now she had become so emotionally involved with her Hauna neighbors that she cried with them in their sorrows and hurts as well as laughed with them in the good times. She realized that the price of any close friendship was vulnerability.

In a few days the village calmed down. Several of the elders came and asked Marilyn to stay because the people needed what she was bringing to them. Marilyn was greatly relieved when the people began bringing their sick to her house again or asking her to come to theirs.

One wizened, little old woman, carrying a sick child in her arms, plaintively asked, "Now, *Apu* Marilyn, you won't pack up and go home? Please, will you stay?"

By this time Marilyn had no thought of leaving Hauna. She hugged the woman's bent frame, put her hand on the child's fevered brow, and said softly, "I'm staying."

With sickness so endemic and epidemics always threatening, Marilyn often felt she was fighting a losing battle. Convinced that many of the illnesses came from the polluted river water, she proposed an ambitious project: the installation of four 2,000-gallon tanks to catch the rainwater and make it available to all villagers.

The only means of getting the huge tanks upriver to Hauna was by stages in four dugout canoes. This process took several weeks. Once the tanks were installed, the people were persuaded to drink only fresh rainwater. Pollution-related illnesses declined.

The classroom under Marilyn's house was now too small for the growing number of literacy students. Hauna began a building program that featured the construction of the largest structure ever built on the "mountain": a schoolhouse, ninety feet long by twenty-four feet wide, containing ten classrooms and a large assembly room.

The village's first schoolhouse took all the Hauna men and Horst Schulz, a Wycliffe support worker, several weeks to build, with the villagers dragging huge logs to the site faster than the carpenters could cut them into planks. Also constructed during 1974 were four other buildings: a clinic, a store, a church, and a translation house. The very size and scope of this building program imparted a sense of permanence, a feeling that literacy had come to stay.

Before opening the school to the whole village, twenty teachers chosen by the village leaders had to prove they were thoroughly grounded in the art of reading and writing their language. After six months of accelerated study and tests, Marilyn felt they were ready.

Twenty-year-old Danny Sauperi, youngest son of Headman Sauperi, was appointed principal. Joel became the assistant. Both had been part of the original group of boys that had shadowed Marilyn from the beginning. They had become dedicated Christians.

The effectiveness of a few teachers had been enhanced by their having been "outside" to work at coffee plantations nearer the coast, where they had picked up some elementary reading skills and a working knowledge of the local trade language, Melanesian Pidgin.

Marilyn was convinced that if their literacy program was to succeed, the whole village, young and old, had to be involved, including some of the influential Hauna elders. Therefore, the school's advisory council, called "the judges," was formed. She reminded these village elders that it was their responsibility to see that the ancient culture of the village was properly protected and preserved. They were proud of this recognition and were enthusiastic advisors.

During every stage of the school's development, Marilyn sought their counsel, explaining, for instance, that it was their responsibility to set the standards for dealing with school disciplinary problems. When one teacher began showing more than academic interest in some of the female students, the council promptly hauled him before the village and suspended him for two months.

The older generation complained, "My head is too hard. The young can learn strange new ways but not the old." But when the older ones eventually discovered they *could* pick out a few words, their joy knew no bounds.

With the aid of the various short-term workers from Ukarumpa operating a donated duplicator, Marilyn began to turn out simple primers for each student. Completing all five primers enabled a student to read and write Sepik Iwam fluently. Those who toted primers became respected for their scholarship.

"Writer's workshops" stimulated even greater motivation. In these workshops students, both young and old, wrote stories about their most exciting experiences. Booklets were written about Sepik Iwam culture, and folklore was gathered from the old men's memories. Village elders enjoyed recounting their hunting and fishing adventures. These stories gave Marilyn more valuable insights into Sepik Iwam life and also added to the reading material available for the new readers. Each story carried the byline of the author. There was even a competition to see who could produce the best story.

She also encouraged the writing of books on how to avoid and treat tropical diseases. Other how-to books illustrated various carved arts and crafts for which the Sepik people were noted. Some booklets described various birds and animals in Hauna. Hymnbooks full of new Sepik Iwam compositions were also printed in the village from stencils.

Except for the primers, books were not given away but were sold for a token charge, either in coins, food, or handicrafts. The amount paid was affordable for even the poorest in the village. The school followed the principle that people only really appreciate those things for which they work or pay. From the funds received, the school began to order other books, usually in English (Papua New Guinea's national language), and assemble a large and varied library.

School lessons included initial theology on the true meaning of Christmas and the life of Jesus, including his death and resurrection. Quietly, often alone, many students asked Papa God to forgive their sins and make them his children. Among the earliest converts were aging Kaku and his wife, Yanomok. Together, they renounced old ways and sought to know Christ's truth. As Kaku held his cherished Yanomok in his arms before her death, she whispered, "It's all right. I'm going home to be with Jesus." She was the first Hauna Christian to die, and her peaceful testimony was a momentous event.

Joel, as young as he was, was gaining unprecedented respect from the village. As a wise and patient teacher, he emerged as, and remains, the spiritual leader of Hauna. Under his leadership, a fledgling church developed and grew week by week from dozens to scores, then to a hundred and more. Hauna Christians learned songs about Jesus and sang them over and over, tirelessly.

At first Joel was reluctant to preach, but Marilyn encouraged him as he prepared his messages. Her greatest joy during Sunday worship was to sit in the little thatched-roof church and hear this intelligent and talented pupil speak of his Lord. His clan members began to recognize him as a man full of God's love.

Joel and Danny increasingly asked for more of God's Talk. They sat by the hour poring over the Melanesian Pidgin New Testament, trying to comprehend its full message.

"*Apu* Marilyn, when are we going to start translating God's Talk into our language? Don't you think you know enough of our language to start?" Danny asked.

"Yes, I think it's time," Marilyn replied that day. "Even though it has been eight years since I arrived, it will still be years before I know all the words needed for translating the New Testament. But God will guide all of us. Let's begin!"

TWELVE

Translation Turning Points

"I was terrified that I would lose my name!" Ronny said.

"Lose your name?" Marilyn asked, "What does that mean?"
"If someone loses his name, it's finished, it's done, it's all over for him."

By 1976 several villagers had been trained to help with the medical work, freeing Marilyn to begin Bible translation full-time. She had a grasp of the basics of Sepik Iwam grammar and an alphabet to work with. There was a nucleus of believers, including Nokiyɨn and the fourteen boys. The time had come to start translating a New Testament book.

Four years before, Marilyn had sat facing the old shaman, Nokiyɨn, and the fourteen preteen boys who had gathered on the bark floor in her house to help her begin translating some stories from the Old Testament and a few New Testament verses.

They had begun at the beginning: Genesis. According to the Hauna creation story, "In the beginning was the crocodile." One clan had descended from the crocodile, another from the python, a third from the cassowary bird, and the fourth from the wild boar.

Verse one of Genesis spoke of Father God, *Adi Komi Winim*, the Creator. Each day as the events of Creation unfolded, excitement increased: earth, sky, fish. Sometimes it took several days for the team to discuss and get a clear grasp of what Marilyn was trying to relate from the verses. Terms like "creatures of the sea" and "livestock" were challenging to explain to a culture unfamiliar with such, and it was often difficult to identify the Sepik Iwam equivalents.

"When do we learn how *Adi Komi* made us?" they each asked repeatedly.

"Just wait. *Adi Komi* still has lots to create before he gets to man."

Each day began with the same question: "Is this the day?"

Finally she was able to answer, "Yes, today is the day."

They aren't going to believe this, Lord, Marilyn prayed silently. *I'll tell them, but then you take it from there!* She drew in a deep breath. "I will tell you how Papa God Creator made man. God came down and scooped up some mud and formed Adam, the first man. Then God blew into his nose, and Adam began breathing." Everyone was so quiet she added, "Dirt and mud—God made man out of this."

The room was totally silent as the expectant group awaited more. Marilyn felt apprehensive. The euphoria about beginning to translate the Scriptures could vanish, she feared, if something in the Bible text clashed with traditional beliefs. All eyes remained fixed on her.

Finally one boy dared to ask, "Is that all?"

"Yes, that's all."

The room erupted with loud discussion, most of which

she couldn't understand with so many talking rapidly, simultaneously.

At last Nokiyin said, "Now we know. We have always wondered if we really did come from the crocodile and python."

The rest of the day Nokiyin and the boys helped Marilyn write the Creation story in clear Sepik Iwam. After that moment the translation team never questioned the Creation story!

As they discussed Adam and Eve's sin, the team came up with the term *dikworaekwobiyie.*

"Wow, that's a long word. Describe what that means," Marilyn said.

"It's stinking, rotten garbage. It means something is bad, no good, wrong, or awful."

"What do you consider a sin?" Marilyn asked. "Tell me the things that everyone in Hauna knows are bad and shouldn't ever be done."

"You should never steal," Tapiya answered.

"It's bad if you kill someone. Some do it, but we know it is real bad," Wokey said.

"I should never tell a lie," Maiyak chimed in, "even though I do sometimes."

Nokiyin added, "It is wrong to sleep with another man's wife."

"And no one should ever, ever show any disrespect toward his elders, especially his mother or father," Moutam told her. "That's really bad."

Marilyn was astounded. *These are five of the Ten Commandments!* "Who told you all these things were wrong?" she asked incredulously.

"Our ancestors," Nokiyin replied. "For generation after generation our fathers have passed down these rules."

Now her unspoken questions were dispelled. The Holy Spirit had shown her that God's laws were indeed written on the hearts of the Sepik Iwam people. Each person was created with the ability to accept God's Word and was given the freedom of choice, with the capacity to believe or disbelieve. Marilyn was not introducing something totally foreign. It had been there; they just had not known the True Source.

As full-time translation continued, curiosity about what was happening in Marilyn's house spread across the village. Unfortunately, most of the older generation were not initially involved because they were embarrassed that they couldn't grasp the concepts and skill of reading as quickly as the young people. Convinced that the adults, especially the leaders, must be involved to produce the best translation possible, Marilyn invited two dozen of Hauna's most prestigious traditional doctors to come each evening and check that day's work for accuracy.

Honored to be needed, these translation checkers called themselves "the judges." They contributed valuable insights and offered important suggestions.

"We are the ones who really know this language," they told Marilyn. "Sometimes these boys give you 'baby' words, so you need us men to give you the acceptable Sepik Iwam vocabulary."

One night after the men had assembled, Paul read the day's translation from Mark 8:23-24: "Jesus took the blind man by the hand and led him out of the village. Then, spitting on the man's eyes, he laid his hands on him and asked, 'Can you see anything now?' The man looked around, 'Yes,' he said" (NLT).

"*Aiyee!*" the resident spitters interrupted. "Jesus did what?"

Paul repeated, "Jesus spit on the man's eyes."

These village leaders, most of them spitters, were astounded by Jesus' healing powers. From that moment on, the Hauna judges more closely identified with Jesus, "The Spitter."

Accepting all the New Testament miracles, the "judges" learned about Jesus' death and miraculous resurrection. These nightly checking sessions, where they heard and discussed God's Word, made a powerful impact on their lives. It would take time, but during the long years ahead, one by one, most of the 160 spitters would become believers.

"Jesus is the greatest spitter who ever lived!" they declared.

Marilyn and the translation crew would often struggle for hours, even days, over a single expression. One such difficult time was searching for the word *soul*. Work came to a complete halt as translators and former spitters brainstormed while Marilyn prayed.

"There is no such word in Sepik Iwam," everyone concluded.

"But there must be one," Marilyn told them. "God has created your language so there must be a word for "soul" because it is a key term in understanding all of God's Word. I must not be explaining it clearly enough." After many hours of discussion, they quit for the day.

That night Marilyn could not sleep. *God, how can we ever declare the gospel without including the word* soul *in your Word?* she anguished. *Please, God! Help us!*

From under her pillow she pulled a chart that listed the

nearly eight thousand verses in the New Testament. The chart also showed how long it would take to complete the translation if they were able to finish ten verses per day, working five days a week. Her original calculations showed that they could have finished the task in five years. But that chart had seen many revisions, and several charts had been made since. Now the new chart was off again because they hadn't translated even one verse that day.

Oh, Lord, I'm so tired of this holy scavenger hunt. This language doesn't even have the words I need to translate your Word. This is an impossible job. I can't do it! I quit!

After her frustrated tears dried, she heard God whisper assurance into her weary soul. *Marilyn, who do you think created this language? I did. I love this language, and I love these precious people. The words are there. Trust me.*

Marilyn met the new day with hope. She didn't want the translation team to feel that their language was inadequate. She knew she just wasn't explaining it properly for them to understand what the term meant. They decided to move on with the translation, temporarily inserting the trade language word *laip*, "life," for "soul" in the manuscript, praying that they would soon find a Sepik Iwam equivalent.

A hunting expedition provided the breakthrough they needed. One Saturday morning Ronny, one of the younger translators, went hunting, leaving at the first touch of daylight with his hunting dog. The jungle was familiar to him since he had been on many hunting forays. Within the first half hour he saw a huge boar that was so busy digging for grubs and roots that it didn't see him.

"He's huge," Ronny whispered to his dog. "Biggest boar I ever saw!"

Usually a boar hunting party included twenty to forty men, who would surround the boar while hunting dogs taunted the animal. The hunters would then hurl their spears at the wild beast. Even though mortally wounded, the boar would charge its tormentors, who would dash for the trees, waiting for the wounded prey to die. Sometimes a hunter would not find shelter soon enough. More Hauna men had been killed by wild boars than by crocodiles and snakes combined.

With foolish bravado, Ronny chased the boar. The startled animal, seeing his adversary for the first time, ran deeper into the dense jungle with the dog and boy pursuing. For more than an hour they chased the boar. Finally totally exhausted, the brave hunter slumped against a tree and watched his pork roast disappear into the underbrush.

"I am too tired to hunt anymore," Ronny told his faithful dog, who also seemed willing to give up the chase.

Clouds had overcast the sky. With no sun to guide him, Ronny had no clue what direction would lead him home. As hunters always did on such occasions, he climbed one of the tallest trees to search the horizon for the river. He looked in all directions but saw no river, only a seemingly unbroken sea of trees. Panic paralyzed him.

Back at the village, late that afternoon, people became concerned. Sunset came, then darkness. People gathered. Worry turned to anguish. Night could only bring death to a young boy alone in the jungle.

At Sauperi's command, huge log drums were beaten, reverberating like thunder through the rain forest, in the hope of guiding the lost boy home. The night passed. The drums grew silent. Like a funeral torch, the sun rose in the sky.

Marilyn, in tears, asked Makapobiya, "What happens when someone is lost and does not return?"

"They are gone from us forever," the old man sadly replied.

The drums beat off and on all morning. There was also death wailing.

Through her years living in Hauna, Marilyn had learned that this situation was rare—nobody got lost in the jungle. Everyone went out daily looking for food, but no one would think of venturing deep into the jungle alone, so no one got lost.

The next morning Andrew and Jonah, two of the translators, headed to the nearby lake, known to be Ronny's favorite hunting spot. They found his canoe but were disappointed when they saw no signs of him.

For long, exhausting hours they took turns blowing a huge shell-horn.

"O Papa God, please let Ronny hear us," Jonah pleaded while Andrew blew. "Please protect him and bring him home."

Their faith and efforts were rewarded. As Ronny had wandered aimlessly that morning, he eventually heard the faint sound and followed the audio beacon back to the lake.

About noon a loud cry announced to the village the astounding news that the three boys had returned. Marilyn hurried to join the crowd that greeted them. The whole village gathered around to hear his story.

"I sat with my back against a tree and kept my dog close to me all night," Ronny remembered. "I didn't let myself go to sleep because I was afraid a large python would swallow me up into his stomach."

"I prayed," Ronny told them. "I asked Papa God to help me find the way home. And he answered my prayers."

"Our prayers too."

"Did you hear the drums during the night?" He hadn't.

While trying to remain on a straight course the second day, Ronny had climbed several trees, looking for the river. After each discouraging climb, he would ask Papa God to guide him. "O *Adi Komi*, I am so lost. Please show me the way back to the river!"

"I was terrified that I would lose my *name!*" Ronny said.

"Lose your name?" Marilyn asked. "What does that mean?"

"If someone loses his name, it's finished, it's done, it's all over for him."

To Marilyn, the expression seemed to refer to dying, but she had already learned the terms for death and dying. The next day she tested the word with the team, reading from Matthew 16:26: "Will a person gain anything if he wins the whole world but loses his [name]? Of course not! There is nothing he can give to regain his [name]" (TEV).

All eyes were bright with discovery. "You mean this is what you've been trying to tell us all these years? Will our name always exist, always going on and on?"

The translation team had been looking for seven years to uncover this concept! The whole translation would have been weak without this idiom. *Name* was the perfect Sepik Iwam word for "soul"!

Marilyn began trying out the expression in other verses: "I will not remove their names from the book of the living. In the presence of my Father and of his angels I will declare openly that they belong to me" (Revelation 3:5, TEV).

As the new idea grew in their minds, they had more questions. Since most non-Sepik Iwam people had difficulty in saying Sepik Iwam names correctly, they asked, "Does God know how to spell my name right? Can he pronounce it right, too?"

"It would be terrible if Papa God couldn't find my name

because it was not written correctly!" they said, referring to Revelation 20:15: "Whoever did not have his name written in the book of the living was thrown into the lake of fire" (TEV).

Marilyn assured them that God made no mistakes. He could pronounce and spell all names perfectly.

God had used a young boy, lost in the jungle, to unlock one of the most important doors for the translation of the Sepik Iwam Scriptures!

THIRTEEN

Spitters to Saints

One evening he lifted his cup following a hearty drink of coffee, laid a hand on his friend's Bible, and said, "Your talk about Papa God is sweet. It is like sugar." He lowered his cup, mused a long moment, then added, "I want Jesus to live in my throat."

Senior citizens played dominant roles in Marilyn's Hauna experience. Prominent among them were Nokiyin, who had adopted Marilyn as his daughter; Makapobiya, whose dying son confronted Marilyn with her first major challenge; and Sauperi, Hauna's headman.

One day as the translation team took their morning break, Marilyn noticed Nokiyin sitting quietly alone. She was struck with the thought that here was someone acutely interested in God's Talk but without a personal relationship with Jesus.

She sat next to him and asked, "Nokiyin, why don't you ask Jesus into your throat?"

"I do want Jesus!" he responded.

With straightforward, childlike faith, Nokiyin asked Jesus into his life as he opened his throat and became an affirmed believer. The old leader's eyes had never sparkled more brightly! There was great rejoicing in Marilyn's heart, too.

Makapobiya, on the other hand, could not point to a specific hour when he committed his life to Jesus. This wise man consistently showed spiritual grace and a radiant attitude. He truly cared about people.

Makapobiya felt that anything written on paper had to be truth, no questions asked. To him, paper with "talk" on it had to be respected and believed.

One morning the translation team discussed the word *mediator*. Divine timing was in evidence again that day. Makapobiya had come, as he often did, to observe and assist. He had just served as a mediator between two fighting clans. A man in one clan had sexually harassed a woman of the other clan. Armed with clubs and spears, the two groups came face-to-face. It was Makapobiya who had stepped fearlessly between them, defusing the conflict. He had served as mediator—*kaaprigi okwowiyin:* the one who brings together.

Makapobiya not only assisted the translation team, he visited Marilyn's house daily. She filled pages of notes gleaned from his stories and explanations of Sepik Iwam customs, such as the incantations of spitters as a part of deathbed procedures. Through his candid explanations of Sepik Iwam life, Marilyn better understood the intricacies underlying the culture.

Maybe he still doesn't think of me as a woman, she wondered, *or perhaps since I'm an outsider, he believes telling me about their social values doesn't break the village code.*

Had it not been for Makapobiya, Marilyn believed that she could never have understood the Sepik Iwam people in sufficient depth to effectively translate God's Talk for them.

Initially, the great man showed no interest in Christianity as a personal faith. He would be a friend, a helper, but for himself he went regularly to the men's spirit house, where they practiced the ways to call on spirits.

But Marilyn began hearing reports of his reluctance to perform the duties of a spitter, although he continued to prescribe natural remedies—an ability in which he excelled. Makapobiya began telling her about his daily conflicts with the grip of evil spirits upon his life. It was a long struggle. Slowly but distinctly, even during his inner turmoil, change came to Makapobiya's personality. He had always been a good man, thoughtful of others, and generous. But eventually his face became bright and seemed less burdened.

Makapobiya finally broke off his practices as a spitter. If someone became gravely ill and summoned him, he called for Marilyn. He might prescribe herbs or medicinal tree bark, but he showed others his respect for Marilyn's blue box of pills and injections. He began inviting people to Sunday services, quoting verses from the expanding New Testament translation and pointedly urging acceptance of Jesus as personal Savior.

When Marilyn commended him one day, he said, "I do these things because I am a Christian." What a thrill for Marilyn to hear him confess his faith.

Under sullen skies on a moonless night, Headman Sauperi visited Marilyn's residence. At the sound of his voice requesting admittance, apprehension gripped Marilyn's heart because of the lateness of the hour. She invited him in. He spoke barely above a whisper.

"Put out the light," he hissed, accustomed to having his every command obeyed. Marilyn dimmed the kerosene lantern, giving the room only faint illumination.

Sauperi held up a smoke-stained basket. "I have something very important and very powerful to show you." He moved his cane chair close to hers and one by one removed fetishes from his basket—boar's tusks, crocodile and cassowary bird bones, skeletal remnants of a human jaw and thigh. He explained the power and function of each item.

To Marilyn it felt like a scene from a scary movie, with a canopy of darkness hovering over the room. *Please, Lord Jesus*, she prayed silently, *you are more powerful than these fetishes. You can command the spirits they serve. Please protect me.*

Picking up her Bible, she said, "This is *Father God Creator's Carving.* It is *his Talk* to all people on earth." Opening to the initial page, she pointed out the words as she began a rough translation, "In the beginning Father God Creator created the heavens and the earth."

Looking intently into Sauperi's face, she continued, "Father God created the crocodile and the cassowary bird. Father God created you." Taking a deep breath, she spoke with increasing boldness, "I am not going to be frightened by spirits because my God is greater and stronger than all of them. Sauperi, you need to ask Jesus into your throat."

Quietly, Sauperi picked up the fetishes and returned them to the basket. He looked at Marilyn a long moment before whispering, "Do not tell anyone about this meeting." He slipped away as quietly as he had come.

Marilyn lay awake through much of that night in lingering shock. Why had Sauperi come? Why had he permitted a woman's eyes to see the fetishes? She had heard that Hauna people believed that if any woman saw any fetish, it would lose its power. Was this perhaps a test for his spiritual powers against Marilyn's beliefs? Trusting that God would prompt her homeland partners to pray, she felt God's peace even though alone that night.

Sauperi came almost daily for visits, sipping *sweet*

water—his name for coffee—and dictating priceless information into Marilyn's tape recorder. He also related blood-tingling accounts of his past experiences as a headhunter.

It was his benevolence and tolerance that had provided the land so Marilyn could live and work above the flood line. At first he was steeped in spiritual darkness, sensing no initial need for carving his talk on the banana leaf, but he still demonstrated an open mind and at times threw the weight of his revered influence behind the project. Eventually his visits with Marilyn increased in frequency as he inquired at length about Papa God's Talk.

One evening he lifted his cup following a hearty drink of coffee, laid a hand on his friend's Bible, and said, "Your talk about Papa God is sweet. It is like sugar." He lowered his cup, mused a long moment, then added, "I want Jesus to live in my throat."

Marilyn rejoiced along with the angels as Sauperi's name was written in the Lamb's Book of Life!

As age impaired his body, Sauperi fell prey to arthritis. He came frequently to Marilyn's house for liniment. As he grew older, he also began to have frequent attacks of pneumonia. Reluctant at first, he at last submitted to penicillin injections. His prompt recovery on each occasion so convinced him of this better way of treatment that he persuaded some of the other jungle doctors to set aside their long-standing prejudice against injections.

During a visit to Ambunti to obtain supplies, Marilyn received a radio call from Joel. "Headman Sauperi has pain in his chest and is having a hard time breathing," he said. "He is asking you to come back and make him well with your medicine."

Sauperi remained conscious until Marilyn returned. She treated him for pneumonia and malaria. However, the following day he fell into a coma. Even though he had a weak but sure pulse and was still breathing, plans began for his funeral. Desperate, Marilyn radioed for advice.

"Your description sounds like cerebral malaria," she was told. "Do you have chloroquine sulfate?"

"Two vials," Marilyn answered.

"Good! One injection should restore him to consciousness within four hours."

When she arrived at Headman Sauperi's residence, one of the spitters was in attendance, and preparations were being made for burial. She took a prepared syringe from her box. As she stepped toward him, however, Sauperi's sons, Joseph and Danny, both professing Christians, blocked her way.

"Please," she urged, gesturing with the syringe. "Your father is my friend. He asked for my help. We must not let him die!"

"Our father is in his death sleep," one of them said. "It is forbidden to give him medicine."

Before he was placed into his grave, Sauperi had died. The entire village went into mourning. Day and night for one week the wailing and weeping continued over the loss of their leader. Marilyn had lost a close friend.

FOURTEEN

We Don't Need Gas— God Is Enough

"You've told us that God knows where we are at all times. He knows we need gas."

"Papa God," she heard one of the men begin to pray. "We are really in trouble. We are still an hour away from our village."

"And mostly we are in big trouble with Marilyn," another added softly.

Marilyn often sought respite on the river. If she used a conventional paddle on her dugout canoe, which she did for short tributary crossings, curious friends would usually follow her. But on days when nerves and energy had been stretched to intolerance, she often cranked up an outboard motor and went speeding across the waters like a vacationer along the southern shore of Lake Michigan.

"I cruise out onto the Sepik," she wrote to friends, "open the throttle, breathe in the fresh air, and thank God for giving me back my convertible! I wish the donors of this boat, the Meloon brothers of Correct Craft in Orlando, could see me now."

As she skimmed over the Sepik River in the speedboat, used mainly as an ambulance, inhabitants from other villages thronged to the shoreline to behold this eighth wonder of the world: a "canoe" traveling at such awesome speed that it even terrified crocodiles!

One morning Marilyn felt she needed a longer break, as well as some supplies from Ambunti, so she foolishly took off by herself on the 110-mile trip.

Wycliffe support workers at Ambunti, Horst and Eugenie Schulz, were surprised to see her arrive late that afternoon.

"What's the matter?" Eugenie asked breathlessly as she rushed outside to meet her.

"Nothing," Marilyn answered casually. "I just needed to get away and get some supplies."

"Did you come all by yourself?" Eugenie's German accent seemed more pronounced as she showed her motherly concern. "What if you had hit a sandbank or had lost a propeller off the motor like before when Judy was with you?"

Horst took up the parental concern. "You really shouldn't have come unless you had sent us a radio message. Don't you remember before, when you hadn't arrived after ten hours, I came looking for you and found you drifting? Or the time I had to rescue you when you got caught in that horrible electrical storm?"

"I hope there are no outboard motors in heaven!" Marilyn sighed. "I've had enough struggle with them to last for eternity."

"How could we have helped you if something had happened today when we didn't even know you were coming our way?"

"OK, I promise I won't do this again. I don't know what I'd do without you two."

When she returned to the village in a few days, she began to teach eight eager apprentices some of the basics of boat maintenance: replacing spark plugs, repairing a damaged propeller, and cleaning the fuel line. They learned what equipment was necessary to take on a trip: extra spark plugs, pins, propellers, a spare fuel line, tools, flashlights, and extra batteries.

The downriver trip to Ambunti in a dugout canoe with an outboard motor required four 5-gallon cans of gas, but it took five cans to fight the current back up the river with a full load.

The speedboat was only used for emergencies because it used more gas and could only carry lighter loads of a couple hundred pounds and four people. However, the forty- to sixty-foot-long dugout canoe could carry a ton of supplies back to the village as well as seven or eight people.

The boys, now ages eleven to eighteen—except Joel who was older—already knew how to read the river better than Marilyn ever would. They were quick to spot shallow areas near dangerous sandbanks and knew how to avoid menacing whirlpools and hazardous submerged logs. Supplies were low, so it was a good time for the eight new "river captains" to try out their skills on the long trip to Ambunti. She summoned the crewmen and delighted them with the announcement of an early morning launch.

Without the responsibility of piloting the dugout over hidden debris and dangerous whirlpools, this trip almost felt like time off for Marilyn. Sitting back in the low rattan chair and armed with a thermos, umbrella, sunblock, and insect repellent, she relaxed and read, reviewed linguistic notes, and just watched the shoreline pass by. Her thoughts roamed, dreaming up ideas to help Hauna people run their own education program and little clinic independently. *Why didn't I turn this job over to the boys years ago?* she wondered contentedly.

The voyage downriver was blissful. Each of the boys took turns guiding the dugout and changing the gas tank when one ran dry. She was especially relaxed when it was Joel's turn to skipper the ship. He was older than the others, cool-headed, capable, and did not think of an outboard motor as merely an adult toy.

"Marilyn!" one teen shouted out. "My stomach is crying for something to eat."

Her sleepy eyes popped open, and she brought out their favorite of her food preparations: peanut-butter-and-jelly sandwiches.

Throughout the trip, one of the boys always perched on the bow, giving added guidance to the driver. Marilyn was relaxed and confident in their speedy and efficient performance of their duties. She could not recall a more pleasant excursion. As she looked at the crew, she silently prayed, *Lord, thank you for these young men. They are so special. Help me give your chosen translators the respect they deserve.*

Visiting Ambunti was in a limited way like reaching Ukarumpa. Marilyn was able to have fellowship in English and be mothered by Eugenie. She also valued the encouragement and special friendship she had with Neal and Martha Kooyers, who also had helped her and Judy in many ways.

Since the river current was very strong near Ambunti, Horst helped tie up and unload the canoe. The outboard motor was removed and stored inside overnight. Eugenie had a huge meal waiting and had arranged accommodations in the guest house for Marilyn's traveling companions.

Items Marilyn had ordered from Ukarumpa had arrived

and were already stacked and ready to be loaded for the return trip the next morning. There were cans of vegetables and packets of dried soups, canned meat, ten 55-pound bags of rice, and six cases of canned fish to feed the translators. More exciting than food supplies, of course, was the mail: bulletins from Ukarumpa, a letter from her church, and three letters from her sister, Shirley.

"Mom and Dad are doing well," Shirley wrote. "The kids are busy with lives of their own now. People at church always ask about you and tell me to remind you that they are praying for you."

As Marilyn put the letter back in the envelope she thought, *I wonder if I could ever convince Shirley to come and help me.*

Everyone was up before dawn for the exhausting job of carefully loading the cargo. The canoe needed to be properly balanced, heavier in the back than the front. Finally, near ten in the morning they shouted their good-byes and thanks to the Schulzes and Kooyers.

"I had hoped to start sooner," Marilyn told the boys. "We won't be home until after dark because it takes at least ten hours to go back upriver."

"We will have a bright moon," Joel said, adding, "and new batteries for our flashlights."

"Plenty of gas?"

"Plenty."

Nightfall comes quickly over the jungle. But on this night, darkness lasted only half an hour when, resembling an over-sized orange, the moon vaulted up before them. Quickly becoming white and bright like a celestial torch, it lit up the river from shore to shore and as far upstream as they could see. Marilyn pulled on a jacket and nestled down into her comfortable chair. Lulled by the purring motor, she fell soundly asleep.

Silence awakened her.

"What's wrong?" she called out.

"The motor is not working."

"Have you checked the spark plugs?" Marilyn asked calmly.

"Sparks OK," the skipper assured her.

"Fuel line dirty or kinked?"

"Fuel line OK."

Silence—except for the lapping of river water against the canoe's sides and the brisk *kyok, kyok* of a night heron.

Marilyn saw a familiar landmark that told her they were less than an hour from home. As she turned her flashlight onto the water, the light reflected off the eyes of a crocodile that was completely submerged up to his eyes. This was his hunting time.

Already the canoe was beginning to drift backward with the current that flowed between three and five miles an hour. Now that they weren't fanned away by the fast motorized travel, hungry mosquitoes swarmed on each occupant like an overstated repellent commercial. She was more than miserable and tired.

Quietly Joel spoke. "I've checked the gas tank. It's empty. All the gas cans are empty, too! We are completely out of strong water."

Marilyn sat upright, exclaiming, "We can't be! It never takes more than five cans of gas from Ambunti to home!"

She looked back and counted the fuel cans. One, two, three . . . four.

"You loaded only four cans of strong water for the trip upriver?" Her voice rose. Anger etched each word. "Why only four? You were told five! When will you learn to follow instructions?"

"Gas costs so much money," they began. "We thought—"

"You thought?" she interrupted angrily. "That's just the problem! You *didn't* think! What are we going to do? You know we can't paddle this heavy canoe upriver. We are less than an hour from Hauna, and now we'll have to drift all the way back to Ambunti. That takes four days!"

"What are we going to do?" she fumed loudly as she swatted futilely at the swarm of hungry mosquitoes.

"Marilyn, sit down," someone said. "Shut your mouth; don't say anything more."

"OK, I can sit here and say nothing, but what are we going to do?"

"We can pray," one ventured.

She slumped back in the chair, silent at last.

"Marilyn, you've told us that God has created everything— the moon, the stars, the sun—and nothing ever falls down. That is a lot of power."

"You've told us that God knows where we are at all times. He knows we need gas."

"Papa God," she heard various ones begin to pray. "We are really in trouble. We are still an hour away from our village."

"And mostly we are in big trouble with Marilyn," another added softly.

"But, Papa God, you said, 'Be there,' and all those stars started shining. The moon tonight, the sun tomorrow. All those things you made never fall down. It takes great power to hold all those stars up above us. If one of them fell, it would kill us and crush every tree."

Marilyn felt a strange calm. She moved for a better look at

the praying crew. They had laid their hands on the motor. Tears flowed hotly down her cheeks.

"Papa God," the prayers continued, "you have much power. Your Jesus walked on the water. What is it for you to make our engine push us home? It would be nothing to you, Papa God!"

"Papa God, you are enough!"

"Yes, you are enough; we don't need any gas!"

The moon was at its brightest, so Marilyn saw clearly as Joel pulled the starter rope. The motor sputtered.

"Please, Papa God! Give power to this motor," he called out.

Joel pulled the starter rope a second time. In an instant the motor started!

"*Aie-yoooh!*" the boys shouted.

As they beat on the sides of the canoe like a huge drum, they shouted, "Papa God! Thank you, this is great!"

"Papa God has power!"

Marilyn thought the motor was running only on a trickle of gas and fumes. As she waited for it to stop, she remembered the time Jesus had used a child to teach a lesson to his disciples, who were worrying about who was going to be the greatest in the kingdom: "Unless you are converted and become like children, you shall not enter the kingdom of heaven. Whoever then humbles himself as this child, he is the greatest in the kingdom of heaven" (Matthew 18:3-4).

And the motor continued running—full speed ahead—all the way home!

The translation team spent long hours at the table, laboring over every verse.

Translation was often fun. Here Marilyn shares a laugh with Lucas and Jonah.

Shirley and Marilyn pose with twin girls named in their honor.

Joel, Hauna's senior pastor, is a respected Bible teacher.

This is but one of five choirs in the thriving Hauna church.

Marilyn, Shirley, and six Hauna men pause on their tour of the USA to meet Dr. Billy Graham and his wife, Ruth.

"Shirley, you can't refuse their gift. This is your first week in the village, and I want them to accept you," Marilyn told her sister.

"OK, but you go first," Shirley said as she handed them to her sister.

Marilyn had eaten many roasted grubs during her years in Hauna but never steamed ones, looking fresh and juicy. With the challenge in Shirley's eyes, Marilyn casually popped one into her mouth. It was too large to swallow whole, so she had to chew it first. The grub was soft and squishy.

As Marilyn smiled and chewed, Shirley saw a bit of green grub juice trickle out of the corners of her sister's mouth. Shirley's eyes widened. Since no one else from the village knew English yet, Marilyn said, "Don't try them, Shirley. I'm afraid I may throw up myself!"

Following a Sepik Iwam custom, Marilyn told their companions, "We're going to wrap these up and take them home with us."

During the next few weeks, Shirley had many other opportunities to sample local delicacies and show respect for the food that was important to Sepik Iwam culture.

Back home Shirley had taught elementary classes, and Marilyn high school. Now Shirley took full responsibility for the younger children and taught as many of the older students as she could, freeing her sister to focus on Bible translation.

Six years earlier Marilyn had begun literacy classes in the evenings in the area under her house. By the time Shirley arrived, the ten-room schoolhouse had been built. Those who had mastered the skills of reading and writing were encouraged to become teachers, instructing four or five others. A few of these new teachers were only eleven and twelve years old! Shirley fine-tuned and expanded the teacher-training program. Some of the more capable teachers were sent to Ambunti Academy downriver, where Neal and Martha Kooyers offered advanced training. Some adults worried that once the young people were exposed to more modern lifestyles, they would opt to leave Hauna forever. Not so with these teachers. They were excited to be a part of the Sepik Iwam education program.

No one was too old or young to be involved if they wanted to be. Various trade skills were requested, like sewing, cooking, carpentry, mechanics, and also sports. Numerous Wycliffe support personnel were willing to come to the village to conduct training workshops.

From the outset, Bible principles and stories became central to Hauna's school curriculum. The Ten Commandments, five of which were already recognized in the Sepik Iwam culture, were the foundation of school discipline.

With her sister's blessing and assistance, Shirley developed an educational program that won government approval; however, her introduction of a grading system met with unanticipated reaction. Sepik Iwam culture considered a grade of B or C unacceptable. Everyone insisted on A's, with the result that some assignments would be done over and over voluntarily until they got their A.

"What do we do about cheating?" Shirley asked one night as she and Marilyn sat by lamplight following the evening meal.

"Cheating?" Marilyn asked, lifting her eyebrow. "Helping each other? In this culture, cooperation is second nature. Why change it in the schoolroom? We need to work within the culture, not against it."

Shirley discovered collaborative learning an effective methodology. It was a rewarding challenge for her to help students develop pride in personal achievement.

"This must be how it sounded in Eden," Shirley mused to Marilyn one evening as the *churr, churr, churr* of a jungle nightjar drifted to their ears from the dark surrounding rain forest. "And the air is so clean."

"I'm glad you've adjusted so quickly."

"Even after all you told me for years, I still couldn't visualize having rapport with students from a different culture. These Hauna kids are terrific. Back home too much of my time at school was spent in discipline. Here, if some kid causes a disturbance, all I have to do is stand back and watch while the other students settle him down. I've never seen people enjoy learning so much. When they finally understand something they've been struggling with, they laugh and cheer as if somebody just hit a home run."

Shirley's arrival also enhanced other aspects of the Hauna ministry. She helped teach an expanded home economics course, using the hand-crank sewing machines already brought to the village. Eventually, 120 older women from all four clans came at various times throughout the week to her sewing classes. When Shirley first arrived, many Hauna girls wore clothing purchased from the village store. She organized the imported patterns, provided bolts of cloth, and taught fitting and sizing. The budding garment makers' response was enthusiastic.

One day several of the young men from the translation team complained to Marilyn, "Why can't we have a sewing class like the women? It doesn't seem fair." Before long the young men were competently sewing shorts and shirts for themselves. From the fabric scraps, they made quilted sheets for cool nights.

Shirley's cooking classes included details on sanitation and public health. Since the Sepik Iwam people originally ate only what they could hunt or find, there were days they went to bed hungry. However, through the years the government brought various foods to the area, such as rice and canned fish, to help supplement their diet. Marilyn and Judy introduced them to bread, which they learned to bake in mud ovens.

Two dozen donated typewriters made a typing class possible. Young and old alike developed typing skills, which eventually enabled the translation team to type the entire Sepik Iwam New Testament.

Shirley encouraged Bible memorization, and during worship services, long Scripture texts were quoted verbatim in unison.

After long days of translation, the teenage translators would often sit around the fires in the evenings and set their favorite verses to music. Through listening to the radio and interacting with other churches farther down the river, they wrote many new choruses, following the rhythm and form of a Melanesian string band.

"I am amazed!" Shirley remarked to Marilyn one day. "I haven't heard anyone sing off pitch or monotone."

"They love music," Marilyn agreed. "Isn't it great to be surrounded by such talent and enthusiasm?"

Being musical, Shirley eventually found herself leading a choir for kids and one for adults. Other choir directors soon emerged, creating several more choirs that involved people of every age.

As well as working with the school, Shirley took a major role in encouraging Joel and Lucas in their evangelistic outreach to other villages. At least once a month, full canoes of witnessing teams visited villages up and down the river tributaries. Specially designed canoes used for this ministry were named *Matthew, Mark, Luke,* and *John.*

Outreach teams continued seeking people more distant from Hauna, sometimes coming upon language groups with as few as fifty speakers. The Hauna Christians had a missionary vision.

"I've just got to turn it in," Shirley sighed over her morning coffee. The sisters were sitting in their cane chairs looking out over the tributary waters.

"Turn what in?" Marilyn asked.

"My ticket."

"I don't know what ticket you're talking about."

"The Lord opened up doors to get me here, and now this is where I'm going to stay," Shirley explained. "I have fallen in love with the people, the work, with everything. I'm going to turn in my return trip airplane ticket."

"Well, praise the Lord," Marilyn said excitedly. "You have fit in here so quickly, and the people love you. Besides, with all the activities and classes you've started, I could never keep them going and also continue translation."

Both sisters had taken the Wycliffe course in jungle medicine. Yet, when it came to medical skills, neither had nursing inclinations much beyond applying bandages or providing Tylenol tablets.

Years before Shirley's arrival, Marilyn and Judy often spent four to five hours each day doing medical work. Then with Sauperi's backing, they had trained several Hauna adults to run a small clinic for treating simple medical problems, freeing the women to work on linguistics and translation. However, there were often serious cases that were brought to them for their advice.

From Shirley's first day in the village, she saw the importance of medical aid in the ministry and from the outset lent a hand. When they ran into major medical emergencies, they would radio Ukarumpa for guidance.

A few months after Shirley came, Marilyn had to be gone from the village. Shirley would remain in Hauna because Sally Entz, Beverly Entz's daughter, had come to stay for six months.

"We'll hold the fort here," Shirley offered. "How long will you be gone?"

"A week and a half," Marilyn replied, "maybe two."

At that moment Shirley's eyes landed on her sister's blue medical kit. She bit her lip lightly and said, "I'll get a taste of what you went through for seven years!"

The first two days following her sister's departure, Shirley helped out with the late-afternoon clinic and, when circumstances required, made house calls. A few sought her services reluctantly since they had never been treated by anyone but Marilyn or Judy for anything serious. But Shirley had the kind of smile that penetrated hearts, and anxieties were quickly quieted.

All went smoothly until Saturday noon. As Shirley and Sally took a break from another hectic morning, they heard wailing in the distance across the river. Then Andrew, one of the translators, came bursting into the house.

"Shirley, Stephen has died!" he shouted frantically.

Stephen, a bright nineteen-year-old, was in her teacher-training classes.

"Is he breathing?" Shirley asked, remembering what her sister had told her about Hauna "deaths."

"Yes, he's still pulling wind," Andrew replied, "so you must come with me! They won't bury him until the morning."

Andrew, Shirley, and Sally went quickly to the shaman's house, where Stephen had been taken. His family members held him in a sitting position, his eyes staring ahead in the grip of a deep coma.

Cerebral malaria, Shirley concluded from the symptoms. *O Lord, help me know what to do.*

Family and clan members were filling the house with wailing.

Sally, perhaps a year older than the sick young man, asked, "What can you do?"

"Let's get back to the radio," Shirley suggested.

But since it was Saturday, their repetitious calls brought no response from their Sepik region headquarters. They used the radio call signs over and over, "Calling Alpha Oscar, Alpha Oscar. This is Alpha Juliet. This is Eighty-six Alpha Juliet, does anyone read me?"

"You stay on the radio," Shirley told Sally. "I'll go back and see if I can help."

Back at Stephen's side, Shirley made frequent pulse checks. The family grew restless.

"*Siya haingikaigik,*" they murmured. ("Plant him.")

Stephen's pulse weakened.

Hour after hour Sally stayed faithfully on the radio. Finally, a little girl at the Sepik region headquarters heard Sally's faint, repeated call and summoned her mother. The woman succeeded in finding a national doctor, who got on the radio with Shirley.

"You must give the boy an injection of liquid chloroquine," he instructed. "If you have it, it will be in a small vial."

Shirley checked her sister's medical box—hypodermic syringes but no vials.

"Lord, help us!" she prayed aloud.

"Please help us now!" Sally added.

Suddenly remembering a rusty bandage box, Shirley hurried to the pantry. Success—three fragile glass vials of the prescribed antimalarial drug.

"Praise the Lord!" she cried aloud.

"How do I get the medicine out?" Shirley asked the others there in the house.

"Marilyn always files the top off," one responded.

While Shirley tried to file off the top of the first vial, the glass shattered, spilling all of the medicine. She was relieved that there were two more. However, she was confused because the doctor had told her how many milligrams to inject, but the vials were marked only with cc's. Not knowing how to convert the dosage amounts, Shirley surmised that she should use the entire vial since there was no way to recap it.

In her nervousness of filling the syringe with the second vial, she pulled back too far and lost the contents of the second vial!

"Oh, Sally! Keep praying because I don't know what I'm doing."

With the last vial in her shaking hands, she successfully filled two syringes.

Darkness had fallen.

Now Shirley couldn't find a flashlight!

Andrew came by canoe to help. Cautiously, step by step, she descended the stairs from her house to the waterside, holding the precious medicine at shoulder height. Trying to step into the canoe in the darkness, she stumbled and fell. Though scratched and bruised, she managed to hold onto the syringes with the last of the precious, life-saving medicine.

The house was packed with wailing people. Mourning cries became deafening. Toby, Stephen's brother, found a dim flashlight and led Shirley closer to his brother's body.

Shirley felt for a pulse in Stephen's neck but found nothing. She put her finger by his nose and couldn't feel any breath. But she felt strongly that God was telling her to give him the medicine.

"Sally, move closer so the shaman can't see what I'm doing."

"He can't see you now," Toby whispered. "Do it!"

For the first time in her entire life, Shirley poised the needle. She had seen her sister give injections, but she had no experience on a real patient.

"Now!" Toby urged.

Half-closing her eyes, Shirley jabbed the needle into Stephen and emptied the contents of the syringe into his body.

Miraculously, a minute later Stephen blinked his eyes, shook his head, and through a dry throat rasped, "May I have a drink of water?"

The wailing stopped abruptly. Shouts of joy filled the house—Stephen had come back to life! The overjoyed family gave him something to eat. In Hauna if you can speak and eat, you are alive.

"I've just seen my first miracle!" Shirley exclaimed. "Thank you, oh, thank you, God, for using me."

SIXTEEN

A Church with No Christians

*"We decided we needed to build a church so Papa God will see
we're ready. We're just waiting now."*

"Look! There it is again."

"I wonder what it is."

"Where do you think it's coming from?"

"What does it mean?"

"When we go down to the big river again, we should ask
our relatives there if they see this light and if they know
what it means and where it is coming from."

High in the mountains, two ridges away from Hauna, a
group of villagers sat huddled around their fire, attempting
to ward off the chill night air. For months now they had
seen a puzzling light in the distance. Some evenings they
could see it, and sometimes they couldn't.

Marilyn and Shirley's house had been built high on the
hill in the middle of the village, with the river tributary

flowing around it. From this vantage point, they could see anyone entering or leaving the village.

Late one afternoon two canoes loaded with men, women, and children cautiously drifted into Hauna. Marilyn immediately knew that the occupants of these canoes were not from anywhere nearby. As she and others greeted the shy visitors, they noticed their lighter skin, their unique style of bush-material clothing, and the rhinoceros beetle horns adorning their pierced noses.

Marilyn invited them up to the house, but communication was almost impossible since the visitors spoke another language and only knew a few Melanesian Pidgin words. Through gestures and observation, the Hauna hosts realized that many of their guests were seriously ill.

Several of the travelers were pitifully thin and coughing: signs of tuberculosis. Marilyn and Shirley recognized yaws, leprosy, and malaria symptoms, too. Most had serious festering sores. When a mother uncovered her baby's back, Marilyn had to dash out to throw up. The baby, they learned, had accidentally rolled into a fire, the burn had become infected, and gangrene had set in. The stench was overpowering.

Later, after everyone had been treated, Marilyn tried to explain to them in the trade language that they must remain in Hauna for at least a month to continue the antibiotics treatment and to regain strength. The spare village house that had been built for visiting government officials was offered them.

Miraculously, the food, medicine, prayer, and love brought healing to each body. None of the guests died. All slowly recovered, even the critically burned infant.

During their month-long stay, the visitors observed firsthand the foreign world of Hauna. When they were strong enough to wander around, they stared in amazement at the clinic that served many other villages and the school with ten classrooms.

They marveled at the church that had been carved out of the hillside, with old canoes providing seats for the worshipers. The visitors' expressions showed that they enjoyed the singing even though they couldn't understand the words, the sermons, or the Sunday school lessons. When the generator was turned on to light the evening church services, the visitors discovered the unknown source of the mysterious light they had seen from their distant village.

In four weeks the mountain guests had learned some Pidgin, and communication had improved. When everyone was well and able to paddle the four-day journey upriver into the mountains, the people of Hauna filled their canoes with huge bags of rice and other provisions for the long trip.

Before they left, the leader approached Marilyn and asked, "Is my talk rubbish? Is my language no good and worthless?"

"No, of course not," Marilyn quickly responded. "God made all the languages. Each one is special."

"Will you come with us and help us?"

"I would come if I could. But I still have a long way to go until God's Talk is translated into Sepik Iwam. I'm sorry, but I can't come right now."

"If our language is worthy of writing, why don't we have someone giving us God's Carving in our language?"

Marilyn found it hard to answer his question. Why didn't they have a translator in his village? "No one knew you were out there," she answered at last.

"When you go back to your birthplace village, will you tell the people there about us?"

"Yes, of course I will," Marilyn assured him.

Sadly the leader asked, "Will you at least come and visit us sometime?"

"Yes," Marilyn promised him, "we'll come and visit. What is the name of your village?"

"Mapisi. Our village name is Mapisi."

"And what is your *tok ples* [language]?"

"Saniyo Hiyewe."

Paul and Joel talked with the people, trying to determine the directions to their village. The hearts of the Hauna Christian community were heavy for the needy mountain people as their canoes pulled away and headed upstream.

"Joel, we need to go to Mapisi," Marilyn announced a few months later. "I've talked to Neal Kooyers, and he wants to go with us on our visit. Since he has been farther up the river than we have been, we need his help to locate the village."

With their dugout canoe full of medicines and food, Marilyn, Shirley, Neal, Joel, and Paul set off early one morning on their expedition. They all hoped that with the aid of the outboard motor, they could make the trip in one day—if they didn't get lost.

Venturing farther upriver than any of them had gone before, they found the scenery breathtaking. Brilliant red flame-of-the-jungle blossoms were everywhere. Tropical foliage, covering the spectrum of greens, and garlands of flowers leaned out to greet them. Panoramic mountain views eventually appeared on both sides of the waterway.

The travelers periodically needed to stop to move fallen logs out of the way or to pull the canoe over rocks. Uncountable little tributaries forked off the main stream, prompting continued prayer for God's guidance. One tributary route turned out to be the wrong choice. Another tributary also grew narrower. Hours passed, and they saw only a few villages. Whenever they asked the curious villagers if they knew where Mapisi was, the name wasn't recognized, so they kept traveling.

Late in the afternoon they spied beached canoes and smoke filtering through the trees ahead. Soon men, women, and children, hearing an outboard motor for the first time by their village, began peering out from the dense rain forest.

Upon landing, the visitors were swarmed with curious pinches. Everyone wanted to feel white skin and straight hair. Neal, standing six feet two inches tall, was a giant. The Hauna men, always living in the tropical sun near the lowlands river, were amazingly black compared to these mountain people.

The five guests were greeted enthusiastically by the leader, who had visited Hauna. He then led them for a half hour deeper into the rain forest, where they came to a small clearing. Most of the village houses were perched high in the trees as protection from invading enemies. A couple of houses on thin, unstable stilts were built close to the ground, but they were in disrepair and obviously unused.

However, at the far edge of the clearing was a sturdy, newly built building on the ground. "What is that building?" Marilyn asked.

"Oh, that is our *sios*," The village leader proudly told her.

"Your church? Do you have a missionary here?"

"No," he answered sadly. "We don't have a missionary yet."

"Has a national pastor come to teach you?"

"No. We don't have any pastor; we have no books. We have no one to teach us," the headman told her.

"Then why do you have a *sios?*"

"When we visited Hauna, we saw everyone going to church. We saw people learning to read God's Talk and singing songs about God and Jesus. When we came back here, we told our people all about your church. We decided we needed to build a church so Papa God will see we're ready. We're just waiting now."

Waiting! Mapisi was just one of many thousands of other villages around the world that were still waiting. Tears filled the visitors' eyes. How long would they have to wait?

Neal was so overwhelmed by the trip to Mapisi that he arranged to have the SIL helicopter air-drop axes, shovels, and bush knives to help the village begin to build an airstrip. Mapisi was so isolated and the river depth so unpredictable that no translation team would be able to live there without the aid of an airstrip.

It took Neal's team three years to complete the project.

Ron and Sandy Lewis had begun linguistic work in 1968 in another Saniyo Hiyewe village twenty-five miles from Mapisi but had returned to the U.S. because of Sandy's near-fatal bout with encephalitis. No one thought they would ever be able to return to village work in Papua New Guinea because of Sandy's weakened condition. However, when they did return years later, Mapisi with its new airstrip became the Lewis's village home.

Although health problems have continued to plague the Lewis family, their projected date for finishing the rough draft of the Saniyo Hiyewe New Testament is early 1999, and they look forward to its dedication in the year 2002.

SEVENTEEN

No, I'm Not Quitting!

*Feeling ashamed of the letter in her pocket, Marilyn fled the
dining room as soon as possible. Back in her room she tore the
letter into shreds.*

A lone figure lay crumpled in front of a freshly carved tombstone. Oblivious to anything around her, the woman on the
ground shook with sobs. The group of people gathering
behind her couldn't help but stand stunned at the raw
emotion being expressed.

Grief. Discouragement. Burnout. Disillusionment. Marilyn had come to a breaking point. She was ready to quit.

A cohesive translation team had been built. The fourteen
boys, now educated teenagers and young men, had
dedicated themselves to the task of seeing God's Talk carved
in Sepik Iwam.

Back in the U.S. a book and two movies about Marilyn's
work were inspiring others to become involved in Bible
translation. On furlough, she had spoken at the Urbana '81
Missions Conference for college students. She and Beverly

Entz had recorded four albums. Like anyone experiencing a great deal of unsought visibility, Marilyn became vulnerable to criticism.

Aware of the attacks, Uncle Cam Townsend wrapped an arm around her shoulder one day and said, "Marilyn, my dear friend, we are counting on you to be big enough to take everything that will come your way."

Because of the close friendship and mentorship Uncle Cam and his wife, Elaine, had with Marilyn, they were her sounding board. In addition, they gave her encouragement for some of her "wild" ideas. During times when she was ready to go into hiding, she would remember Uncle Cam's words. She could never disappoint him.

With her high level of visibility, she had become oversensitive to the stress of trying to please everyone. Although an impossible feat, she felt that she must work harder not to disappoint anyone trying to be a flawless representative of Wycliffe and the Papua New Guinea branch to the many Christian partners across the U.S.

Uncle Cam's "homegoing" on April 23, 1982, knocked an immense hole in Marilyn's emotional support foundation. When she felt she needed his encouragement the most, he was gone.

She reached her lowest point a couple of months later while at Waxhaw, North Carolina, at the Jungle Aviation And Radio Service (JAARS) Center, a sister organization to Wycliffe. Even though she had numerous friends cheering her on, and though she was completely committed to the work of Wycliffe, Marilyn began to entertain thoughts of withdrawing from the struggle. She decided she couldn't take the pressure.

She also couldn't help but be discouraged thinking about her unfulfilled translation goal charts, which showed how many years it would take for her to finish. The current chart with her latest calculations was discouraging. She still had so many years to go until the Sepik Iwam Bible translation would be completed.

She felt she couldn't go on. Taking pen and paper, she scribbled out her resignation. With the rough draft of the resignation in her pocket, she wandered over to the lodge's dining room for a cup of coffee. Sitting there was Elaine Townsend, who motioned for Marilyn to come join her. Marilyn hesitated momentarily, fearing tears would start to flow. But how could she be rude and brush off the invitation?

"Good morning, Marilyn," Elaine greeted her cheerfully. "How are you this beautiful morning?"

"OK," Marilyn lied, "and you?"

"I'm fine, thank you. Do you want to hear some exciting news?"

"Sure," Marilyn managed to say.

"Well, I've just confirmed my plans to go to Brazil to encourage our members there, and . . ."

As Elaine continued to share her future plans, Marilyn was struck with the thought: *Here is a woman who just lost her husband two months ago. But is she feeling sorry for herself, ready to quit and pull away from her visibility? No! She's pressing forward with the plans that she and Uncle Cam had made together!*

Feeling ashamed of the letter in her pocket, Marilyn fled the dining room as soon as possible. Back in her room she tore the letter into shreds. She had been reminded that she wasn't the only one in Wycliffe who had ever felt discouraged. Everyone had times like this.

She remembered a statement from a translator friend: "Whenever there is a completion and dedication of another New Testament, it is nothing short of a miracle." Marilyn still wanted to be part of a miracle.

She needed to talk to Uncle Cam. His grave lay between the Museum of the Alphabet and the Mexico Cardenas Museum at the JAARS Center. She practically ran across the street to his grave and sank to her knees. She reread the tombstone inscription:

> William Cameron Townsend
> July 9, 1896—April 23, 1982
> Dear Ones: By love serve one another,
> Finish the task, translate the Scriptures
> into every language.
> Uncle Cam
> Beloved Husband, Father, and Grandfather

Marilyn began weeping. Through her sobs she called out in a loud voice, "Uncle Cam, I'm not quitting!" Raising her hands heavenward she kept saying, "Do you hear me? I'm not going to quit!"

Unknown to her, a guide for a museum tour was about to point out Uncle Cam's grave to a group of visitors.

"O God," she prayed loudly, "please give me the strength to fulfill my promise to you and to Uncle Cam."

As she knelt by the grave, God's comfort and peace wrapped around her heart like strong arms, providing the direction she needed. She was reminded again that the commission God had given her was possible in *his* strength, not her own. And so she got up and headed back to Papua New Guinea.

EIGHTEEN

Sharing the Load

"Every day seemed to be a new adventure as we watched the crew of teens and villagers perform the impossible."

"Steel doesn't float! Everyone should know that. If the head of my ax accidentally falls out of my canoe, it sinks to the bottom of the river. This huge steel boat will sink to the bottom of the river, too."

No one in Hauna believed the large metal boat would ever sail the Sepik River. Despite their doubts, scores of Hauna craftsmen worked for three months alongside Dean Puzey and George Tilt. Dean, a farmer and the inventor of the Walk-about Sawmill, popular in Papua New Guinea, was a frequent visitor to Hauna. He designed the forty-eight-foot metal pontoon craft in a scale grander than Marilyn's early dreams. George joined the project and spent weeks helping Dean weld it together.

"It's too big."

"It's too heavy because it's steel!"

On March 3, 1984, twenty tons of donated steel landed in Wewak, the northwestern seaport of Papua New Guinea.

This was the beginning of a seemingly impossible assignment: transporting tons of steel to Hauna and creating a river craft in the middle of the jungle.

After being transported for five hours over mountain roads from Wewak to the Sepik River, the inconceivable task was to load six outboard canoes with twenty tons of supplies. The logistics of moving the steel down the muddy riverbanks and onto the canoes was nothing short of genius. Thirty of Hauna's strongest men impressed the American helpers with their strength, ingenuity, and teamwork. None of the steel landed irretrievably at the bottom of the river.

The six canoes, powered by twenty-five-horsepower outboard motors, traveled upriver for eighteen hours. Then the workers were met by the same backbreaking chore, only in reverse—getting the tons of material up a muddy bank to a flat area, where it would be welded together into a steel boat.

All of Hauna considered this boat construction the most astonishing feat they had ever witnessed. A craft forty-eight feet long, twelve feet wide, and two decks high, designed to carry six tons or one hundred people, was mind-boggling. During its construction, people sat together long after sunset, discussing the crazy men who had come to build a boat that could not possibly float.

Finally the day came to test the buoyancy of the two welded pontoons, each weighing over two tons. The slope down to the river was doused with water, turning the ground into a slick mud-way. Over one hundred men strained to pull and shove each pontoon down to the water. Hauna's residents lined the riverbank. Skeptical that these monster inventions would actually float, they wanted to witness the sinking.

Perched on the first pontoon were Marilyn and Shirley. When the village women realized that they were planning to stay on board all the way down the muddy bank into the river, they began to shout their warnings.

"Jump off!"

"You're going to sink with the big canoe. Get off now."

As the weight of the pontoon plunged the nose into the river, the pontoon did get washed with water several feet deep. Securely seated back from the front edge, Marilyn threw up her arms and cheered.

Once the pontoons were fully on the river, they rose majestically with barely seven inches of draft. Everyone was amazed; even the canoes sat deeper in the water than that.

The roar of amazement and delight from the village was deafening. Right before their eyes, a craft of immense proportions, made out of steel, floated regally in their own village.

Placed on the front of the boat was the inscription: "That the word of the Lord may speed on and triumph" (2 Thessalonians 3:1, RSV).

In December that year, the *Sepik Queen* made several trips up and down the river, bringing hundreds to the first Hauna Crusade. Altogether, twelve hundred people attended. They learned of Jesus' payment for their sins, and dozens turned their lives over to Jesus. Through its many years of service, the *Sepik Queen* has carried supplies for the village store, school, and church and brought to Hauna hundreds of visitors from around the world. Although too large to go into the smaller tributaries, especially during dry season, the *Sepik Queen*, as a traveling clinic, has dispensed medical care along the river.

Missionaries come in different age groups, the sisters learned.

"I'm looking for projects that could involve one of our

summer teams," Bob Bland, founder of Teen Missions International, explained to Marilyn over the radio one day. "Each summer we train nearly two thousand young people in basic skills like carpentry, laying cement blocks, and pouring concrete. Then we divide them into teams of about thirty-five and send them out on assignments all over the world. They construct churches, schools, and medical clinics. They also build roads, cut out airstrips in isolated jungle locations, or do whatever is needed that will glorify the Lord."

"These are teams of guys?" Marilyn asked.

"Both guys and girls," Bob responded. "We've got girls who can lay a string of blocks as straight as a professional mason. Do you have any projects that could use one of our teams?"

"We desperately need an airstrip," Marilyn said, dreaming.

"Let's send a bunch of kids next summer to build one for you!"

Mid-1985 in Wewak, Marilyn and Shirley met the crew of thirty-five North American kids, ranging in age from thirteen to nineteen, with their leaders. The twenty-three hour trip to Hauna included a trek by truck over rough mountain roads and fifteen hours of travel on the Sepik—much of it at night.

"Did you say there are real crocodiles in this river, Shirley?" a girl from New Jersey wanted to know.

"Hundreds of crocodiles," Shirley replied.

"And pythons?"

"Pythons live in the jungle, but we do have a few in the thatched roof of our house."

"Will we see one?"

"Count on it."

Under the supervision of Stan Straughan and David Moore from Teen Missions, over one hundred Hauna workers and the teens cut a strip into the dense jungle. Massive trees had to be felled and removed. Not one root could be left because if even one remained, it would rot and eventually create a soft spot, which could cause a serious accident during landing. Marilyn and Shirley joined all the village women as they raked the last debris and carted it all away in bark baskets. It was unheard of to construct an airstrip in Papua New Guinea in only two months!

After the initial airstrip construction crew, other teams from Teen Missions came to Hauna every summer. A new translation house, school buildings, and facilities for gathering clean rain water for Hauna and for distant villages are among the projects the teens completed.

In the spring of 1987 an even more challenging and impressive task began. The project involved a large helicopter hangar that had been donated by a departing Dutch oil exploration company. Stan Straughan accepted the challenge to work with sixty Hauna men to disassemble and transport the three-story-high structure upriver four miles to the village.

Hauna men perched on top of the thirty-foot-high hangar and struggled to loosen the huge bolts. The framing included thirty-two massive I-beams weighing thirty pounds per foot, some measuring up to sixty feet in length. There were several near-tragic accidents, but fortunately no serious injuries.

Next came the challenge of hauling the metal roofing and I-beams to Hauna. It took sixty people two days per beam to transport each piece from the hangar site, down the muddy embankment to the strapped-together canoe-barge, up the river four miles, then off the canoes, up the slippery bank, and along the half-mile path to the future reconstruction site. If one of the I-beams had slipped into the river, it would have been impossible to rebuild the structure.

That summer a Teen Missions crew joined the local men. Using Bob Bland's ingenious A-frame invention for a derrick, the impossible was accomplished—with no modern machinery.

Over the next five years, the abandoned hangar was rebuilt into a jungle hospital. Funding for the clinic came from various groups. Franklin Graham of World Medical Missions sent the needed setup equipment, including operating room necessities. MAP International provided the medications through the financial help of a generous group of physicians in Chattanooga, Tennessee, organized by Dr. Bruce Marsh. A second floor was later added, allowing critically ill patients to remain at the Center until they were well enough to travel home.

The completed health clinic in Hauna, serving over five thousand people up and down the river, is one of Papua New Guinea's tallest buildings outside the capital of Port Moresby. Daily, approximately 125 patients come through the Hauna Health Center. Marilyn was amazed at the way God networked Bob Bland, Stan Straughan, and the Teen Missions teams with the East Sepik provincial government's plans for a medical center in the Hauna district.

Through partnership with the other mission organizations, these projects took shape while the translation team continued toward their goal of completing the Sepik Iwam New Testament.

Termites in Hauna feasted on the old posts of the school building that had been built with jungle materials, except for the metal roof that caught rainwater. Eventually the supporting posts wobbled dangerously.

Coming to the rescue were Noah and Alta Miller from Hartville, Ohio. Also joining the team were Owen and Lorene Coblentz and their daughter, Elena. For seven months they helped Hauna build their new school building, with every plank used in the building coming from the surrounding jungle.

The proud new school was 145 feet long, forty-five feet wide, and two stories high and boasted twenty-one classrooms and a library filled with books in Sepik Iwam, Melanesian Pidgin, and English, Papua New Guinea's national language. Most of the students eventually learned how to read and write in all three languages.

In the next few years Noah Miller returned to Hauna five times to help with other construction projects and brought with him teams of builders from Ohio. Without the scores of Wycliffe support members from Ukarumpa and the hundreds of guest helpers, young and old, none of these Hauna projects could have been accomplished.

NINETEEN

Calling On a Greater Power

"The wind, Papa God, turn the wind around," Joel prayed.

"Fire!"

It had been a calm, quiet day. The translation team was concentrating on the day's verses. In the next room two visiting women, Judy Anderson and Anne Thomas, were typing and proofreading stories.

"FIRE!"

Everyone jumped. Michael's chair slammed to the floor. Danny ran out of the house so fast that it seemed as if he'd gone through the wall. The other translators were right behind him. Two men working under the house jumped up so fast they almost knocked themselves out. Marilyn and the other women ran frantically through the house. Realizing it wasn't their own home on fire, they dashed outside, half fell down the hill, and scrambled through the jungle to the other group of dwellings. Fire in a village, where the dry sago palm thatched-roof houses huddled close together, usually meant disaster.

People from all parts of the village poured out of their houses, taking up the shout. Most of the people still thought fire was an avenging spirit, visited upon households at some sorcerer's call.

The heat from the blazing house was so intense that it was impossible to get close enough to rescue the family's possessions before the house burned to the ground. A strong wind was blowing sparks toward seven other houses built in a row. Already, fingers of flame were reaching out from the burning house toward the next one. People all along the row were frantically throwing things out of their homes. Men perched on top of each house, watching for sparks flying in their direction so they could quickly extinguish any that landed.

Bunched together facing the flames, a group of Christians were crying and wailing, holding on to each other for support. Then above the pandemonium, Joel's strong voice rang out.

"O Papa God, all of our things are in our homes: our axes, our bows and arrows, spears, and bush knives. The wind, Papa God, turn the wind around," Joel prayed. "You are the Strong One. You are stronger than the wind."

"Yes, Papa God, please turn the wind around," others agreed.

Miraculously, the direction of the wind *did* change. The other houses were saved. God's awesome power smashed the destructive powers at work that day in Hauna.

Smoky silhouettes of men swayed and twitched as they sat in a circle by the flickering firelight. Moans punctuated with cries of pain accompanied an ancient ritual.

For generations in Hauna, young men reaching the age of

puberty would gather on a specified night with powerful spitters to begin their training in the ways of the village spirits. Most people groups along the Sepik River constructed long "men's houses," where traditional secrets were passed to the next generation.

Joining the circle of shamans and novices were two young translators, Paul and Jonah. Several of their friends had encouraged them to join the training session that night. Curiosity about the training in spells and magic prompted them to attend together. At this point in their Christian experience, they were unaware of the dangerous situation they were now in.

Following the shamans' instructions and chewing the gingerroot plant, which they were told contained a powerful spirit, the young boys called out for spirits to possess them. As arms and legs of others around them began to jerk and quiver, Paul leaned over to Jonah and whispered in his ear, "Is anything happening to you? Are your legs moving?"

"No, I don't feel a thing," Jonah answered. "Nope, nothing is moving."

"Same with me. *Kiya!*" Paul expressed his disapproval more loudly. "Hey! There isn't a true power here. Jesus' power can win over this."

"Let's get out of here, what do you say?" Jonah suggested.

Jonah and Paul took an unheard-of step of boldness and faith. In front of powerful shamans and dozens of boys their own age, they resolutely walked out.

Jonah became firm in his stand as a Christian. He knew that Jesus' power was stronger than that of the jungle spirits, and he was bold in proclaiming it.

Above the jungle symphony one night, Jonah heard the

familiar sounds of a spitter. Moaning and crying, the traditional healer labored to become possessed by a spirit, believing the spirit could help him determine what was causing the sickness in his patient.

Jonah got out from under his mosquito net, went to the door of his house, and shouted into the darkness. "*Harimwo!* Listen! In the name of Jesus I want to tell you that this power that you are calling on is not enough! Jesus' power is far and above everything, and it can put down Satan's work."

At the mention of Jesus' name, the spitter in the nearby house immediately lost his demon-possessed state. Everything became silent, and Jonah crawled back under his mosquito net and fell asleep.

Twin births were not welcomed in Hauna. Tradition taught that the second child had been conceived by an evil spirit, so it must die. A mother wouldn't feed or care for the second-born twin, allowing it to die. Sometimes she would place it in a basket and allow it to drift away on the river. If the mother died giving birth to twins, both babies would be buried alive, next to their mother.

When Joel's wife, Priscilla, gave birth to twin girls, they named the two Marilyn and Shirley. As pastor of the church, Joel took a stand with his wife against an uproar of opposition from those in the village who predicted trouble for their family if they didn't get rid of the second born.

Little Marilyn and Shirley were thriving, attractive, intelligent babies. They were so identical that it was a challenge to tell them apart. Dropping in for a quick hug from the two darlings became a regular habit for their adult namesakes.

Two years later a whooping-cough epidemic swept

through Hauna. Marilyn and Shirley worked tirelessly day and night that week, going from house to house to teach the mothers how to remove phlegm from young throats. As the illness ran its course, twenty-two children died, including Joel and Priscilla's little Marilyn.

Exhausted from days with little sleep, Marilyn sobbed, "Lord, why did you allow her to die? Here is a couple who stood up for you against the fear and superstition of the whole village!" This was one of the saddest and most difficult moments Marilyn and Shirley had experienced during their time in Hauna.

Instead of applying white mud, which was once used to prepare a body for burial, the family used baby powder before wrapping the child in bark. As Joel and Priscilla stood by the grave, hecklers taunted, "We told you so!" But when Joel began to pray, the crowd became silent. It was the first time anyone had ever prayed at a graveside.

"Papa God, I am not angry," he began. "I know our little Marilyn is with you in heaven. You don't make mistakes. Satan is not going to win here. I will not turn my back on you. I will keep believing. You are the Strong One above all things." His voice choked with emotion as he continued, "My little Marilyn is in a better place than here. I think, Papa, you wanted her with you, so I am OK. I am OK, Papa."

Beside that fresh little grave, Marilyn and Shirley witnessed again that the Bible was being carved onto more than just banana leaves in Hauna village—God's words were being written upon human hearts.

..

TWENTY

Jude 25

*Excitement was running high among the translators.
This could be a historic day for Hauna, but it was their secret;
not even Shirley knew.*

This could be the day. They had all checked their calculations the night before. Barring any difficult verses or terms, it might be possible.

In the early morning light, Marilyn pulled out her progress chart from under her pillow. Six months ago she had projected that they might finish the rough draft on July 24, 1988. She had secretly hoped they could shave off two days, giving her the best birthday present of her life.

But today was June 24, a month early.

As usual the wake-up aroma of coffee filled the air of the translation house as everyone arrived for their morning devotions together. Andrew and Hosea with their servants' hearts were first, getting the cups and cookies ready for the others. None of the translators was late this morning.

Daily devotions at 7:30 A.M. included the translation team and the work crews from the school, clinic, sawmill, and airstrip, along with the carpenters, mechanics, typists, cleaning women, and cooks. Excitement was running high among the translators. This could be a historic day for Hauna, but it was their secret; not even Shirley knew.

As the rest of the workers filed out, Danny and Jonah raced for another cup of coffee and begged Hosea, the keeper of the cookies, "We need two more cookies today. It's a special day."

The team of fourteen translators lined both sides of the long work table. Marilyn took her place next to Paul, who was the scribe. Throughout the years of translation work, Paul had faithfully recorded the rough draft of the verses completed on each day. Next to Paul was Tom, bright and serious, who filled in very capably whenever Paul couldn't do this job.

Across from Marilyn sat Joseph, Headman Sauperi's oldest son, government councilman of the village. Outspoken like his father, he was always in the middle of any decision-making process. Next was Toby, a faithful pastor with a quiet and agreeable personality. He was always consistent in his lifestyle and Christian testimony. Timoti was next. He had survived polio as a baby. During Marilyn's early years in Hauna, he was the dedicated volunteer who transported her around the village in his canoe.

Hardworking Silas was always willing to help out whenever needed. Philip, with a quiet, positive nature, was the chief maintenance man for water systems and plumbing.

Across from Philip was outspoken Gideon, opinionated and always ready for a rousing debate. Like Timoti, he had helped in countless ways. He had been among the first to help with the medical work. Next to him was Danny, Sauperi's youngest son. Honest and fair and very organized, he loved making and following lists. He became the first principal of the school.

Next at the table was gentle and humble Jonah, Paul's best friend. He and Michael would sit for hours in front of the computer, entering the newly translated verses. Michael, very dedicated to the village program, never allowed his speech impediment to deter him; he later became a school principal.

Besides being part of the translation team, Ronny, who sported a dry sense of humor, was also one of the village pastors. His love for hunting in the jungle had sometimes lured him from the translation table.

Sitting at the other end of the table was Joel, older than the rest and the uncle of most of the other translators. Hauna's senior pastor, he possessed a unique gift for counseling.

Andrew joined the others at the table after helping clean up. Gifted with a happy disposition, he seemed to end up with the least desirable jobs yet did them with a smile and not a word of complaint.

Marilyn's thoughts moved to the dedicated faculty who worked with Shirley in the school and who also had become key players in the final stages of the New Testament translation. Zechariah had been only four years old when Marilyn arrived but was a young man now. Shirley recognized his scholastic ability and relied heavily on him for the correct Sepik Iwam grammar as they began creating new primers.

Lucas began to play a significant role with the translation team after he returned from three years at the Christian Leadership Training College in Papua New Guinea's highlands. Wilson and Morrison, also significant assets, had attended Wewak Teacher Training College, where they earned government certification. Rarely do men this highly trained return to their village. The Hauna schools and the translation process were doubly blessed.

With a number of well-educated assistants, an assembly line for translation and checking had been formed. The work team was split into pairs, with the partners bringing their completed verses back to Paul and Marilyn to record and review. Then the whole group met together for discussion and revision. The agreed-upon translation then moved to the computer typists.

"Lord, you know how each one of us has given up, several times," Marilyn prayed. "Thank you for keeping this incredible team moving forward through it all."

Jude—the last book to be translated into Sepik Iwam—only twenty-five verses. Five of the most difficult words to translate, which had taken years to find, were there in the first few verses—mercy, peace, love, salvation, and faith. A flood of memories rushed in as they recalled the hours, sometimes days, of discussion to settle on the proper Sepik Iwam expression for these key terms.

Verse two: "May mercy, peace, and love be yours in full measure" (TEV).

Michael, stuttering in excitement said, "Remember when we settled on *naingwobumbu* for the English word "mercy"? At first we didn't think we had a word like this."

Toby added, *"Naingwobumbu*, we deserve to be punished, but because of God's overabundance of kindness, he doesn't want to harm us. Through his compassion and pity for us, God forgives us."

"It took us nine long years to come up with a word for 'forgiveness,'" Marilyn recalled. "I'll never forget the dedication service for this main house when everyone circled the building and then put their arms around each other. I had never seen that happen before. You explained that putting your arms around another indicated a desire for reconciliation, which is forgiveness, *haiyoprimdiyiumiigi*."

"*Nongwomamairae* is how we say 'peace,'" Silas continued. "This was one of the easier words to translate since our history is full of fighting. We are always looking for a settlement. We often say that our stomachs and throats must be easy, which means 'peace.'"

"We always knew that our language was a much better language than English that only has one word for 'love,'" Ronny teased. "Here in verse two of Jude, we will use the word *naingwokwonanae*. But when we translated Matthew 22:37, we used *mhii kwoinim mi kiriirkirieya* because there it talks about loving God with our whole heart, soul, and mind."

"'Stomach, throat, strongly loves' for that verse in Matthew," Tom said.

"Loving money uses another word, *naingwokwonanaeiyim*," Paul added. "When money came into our lives, it gave us a certain amount of new power, but it also brought us a lot of trouble. Why? Because we loved it more than we loved God."

"*Kiya!* Let's move on to verse three," Danny interjected. "Stop talking so much. We want to finish today. 'My dear friends, I was doing my best to write to you about the salvation we share in common.' At least we didn't have to discuss how to say the word 'salvation.'"

"We discovered this word when someone almost drowned, and we realized this is what God did for us through Jesus," Andrew answered. "*Nanmaiwarkainaim*—salvation—God rescues us with his net to save us from going under."

"And then there's *wakaeyokna apim* for 'faith,'" Joseph

said. "This word explains that our thinking and our throats are now joined."

It was getting dark; the translators were working late. They came to the last two verses of the epistle of Jude:

"AND NOW, ALL GLORY TO GOD, WHO IS ABLE TO KEEP YOU FROM STUMBLING, AND WHO WILL BRING YOU INTO HIS GLORIOUS PRESENCE INNOCENT OF SIN AND WITH GREAT JOY. ALL GLORY TO HIM, WHO ALONE IS GOD OUR SAVIOR, THROUGH JESUS CHRIST OUR LORD. YES, GLORY, MAJESTY, POWER, AND AUTHORITY BELONG TO HIM, IN THE BEGINNING, NOW, AND FOREVERMORE. AMEN" (NLT).

A detonation of emotion shook the translation house at Hauna village. Laughter and tears erupted simultaneously. It had taken 7,305 days—1,043 weeks—to complete this miracle of Bible translation. Two decades! Twelve years prior to the end of the century, a rusting typewriter clicked the culminating words needed to complete the first draft of the New Testament in the Sepik Iwam language.

Marilyn raced to the kitchen and outfitted each of the translation team with a metal pot or pan and a spoon as a drumstick. As they marched in celebration through Hauna, it wasn't long before everyone knew the impossible task had reached a major milestone. The men were jumping into each other's arms and shouting. The rest of the village came out of their homes to join the surprise celebration.

Shirley, her throat tight with emotion, managed to say, "What if I hadn't stayed? I would have missed this moment with all of you."

"I just wish everyone who had a part in making this possible could be here to rejoice with us," Marilyn responded.

The sisters gave each other a high five.

Even after the first draft of the New Testament was completed, the patience of the team would still be tested during the following weeks and months. First, Marilyn and the team leaders would analyze the yet unchecked Scripture portions with Wycliffe translation consultants at Ukarumpa to assure correct biblical meaning from the Greek. Next they would face galleys and page proofs. Since the people wanted both Sepik Iwam and English versions included, extra time would be required to align the two translations on each page. Team members would design the cover. Printing would eventually be done in Hong Kong.

But today would be a day of celebration. The impossible had just become possible.

TWENTY-ONE

Six Hauna Men in a Flying Canoe

"C'n ah he'p yuh?" the girl behind the counter asked.

Shocked, Paul turned to Marilyn. "What language do they speak here?"

"English," Marilyn answered, "but sometimes very different sounding."

"*Apu*, for years now we have known you and Shirley, but we have never seen your birthplace in the United States," Ronny said.

"You have shown us pictures of the people and churches who have supported you with their prayers and money. It will be so good to be able to thank them personally for making it possible for us to have God's Word in our own heart language," Joel added.

With the assistance of clan leaders, a team of six men was chosen. Some had English language skills that would be needed for the trip. Michael, who suffered from an acute-stuttering syndrome, disqualified himself. A remarkable sense of maturity and fairness prevailed. Reviewing a world map in one of the schoolrooms, a few who had never ventured beyond Sepik waters cringed at the prospect of such a long journey.

During the orientation sessions the men asked innumerable questions about U.S. culture. They wanted to be sensitive to the foreign customs so they wouldn't be offensive in any way. Being raised in a culture with exact opposite manners toward women, they were baffled at why an American man should offer his seat to a woman or why he should hold open a door to let a woman enter a building first.

In December 1988 the eight travel mates, Marilyn, Shirley, Jonah, Joel, Ronny, Paul, Zechariah, and Lucas, boarded a Qantas Boeing 747, fastened their seat belts, and sat in sober silence as roaring jet engines thrust the massive aircraft into the sky toward Los Angeles.

"We are flying," Paul said with a nervous cough.

"Isn't this dangerous?" Joel asked.

"We are ten times safer in this jet," Shirley assured him, "than we are when we're riding in the back of one of those four-ton trucks in Wewak!"

"White mountains," Ronny said, venturing a look out the window.

"Actually, those are clouds."

"We're flying higher than the birds!" Lucas exclaimed.

Various aspects of international airline routine evoked puzzled faces: hot towels, cool towels—carried on trays and served with tongs? Mealtime was the next wonder. Steaming hot food was brought to each of them. Although no one had much of an appetite because of their excitement, they ate for the sheer novelty of being served food in an airplane.

A two-day stopover in Honolulu gave the men their first view of high-rise buildings. Their motel rooms were on the fourteenth floor. This was the first time they had seen a building this tall, let alone stood on a floor so high off the ground. No one could sleep that first night.

"How many generators do they need to keep all these lights going all night?"

Having no concept of how many cars there were in Honolulu, they asked, "Why do those same cars keep driving around and around this building?"

The team's first program was scheduled at the Waikiki Baptist Church. The audience was electrified as the Hauna men made a dramatic entrance into the sanctuary, beating drums, dressed in typical jungle regalia, faces painted in celebration colors, and traditional spears held in readiness for the hunt. Several of the men told how God's Talk had changed their lives. As Marilyn glanced at the audience, she knew the U.S. tour would be well received.

Los Angeles provided its share of culture shock. They landed at five o'clock, the peak of evening rush-hour traffic. Wycliffe headquarters sent a van to pick them up. As they pulled onto the freeway, they promptly encountered gridlock and traveled at a snail's pace, bumper to bumper, six lanes headed north, six lanes south.

"I can paddle my canoe faster than this!" Jonah quipped.

"We'll never get out of here," Paul added, a bit nervous. "We're trapped!"

As they inched past a large car lot, Shirley pointed out, "Those are cars for sale."

Thinking the "84" painted on the window was the price, not the model's year, Lucas was astounded, "Hey, cars are cheap in this country."

"All of those cars are for sale?" Joel marveled. "There's no space for any more cars here!"

Thinking that all roads were like the Los Angeles freeway at rush hour, Joel added, "I'd like to talk to your prime minister. He shouldn't allow any more cars to be made until they finish with all these on this road."

At this point Marilyn and Shirley realized there were many things they hadn't prepared these Hauna travelers for.

Eventually turning onto a less-traveled freeway, the van headed for Huntington Beach and the main offices of Wycliffe Bible Translators. Here, welcomed with love and enthusiasm, the travelers put aside their culture shock to meet their American brothers and sisters.

Even with their hearts warmed by the greeting in California, the group was ill-prepared for Midwest weather. A raging blizzard had almost closed Chicago's airport the day they arrived. The windchill temperature had plummeted to twenty degrees below zero.

The tropical visitors were greeted by Marilyn and Shirley's family, who had brought coats, hats, and gloves. Lured by a desire to be first through the automatic doors, Lucas politely refused a coat and grabbed a couple of suitcases. With youthful bravado, he darted out of the baggage area into a frigid blast. He halted in shock. Bellowing as he dashed back inside, his eyes were wide with disbelief. He warned his friends, "We'll die if we go out there! It's worse than burning to death! That wind cuts like knives." Everyone was convinced to wear the foreign winter gear.

Marilyn and Shirley had scheduled the winter months of the tour in the southern states. As they drove south, even Lucas began to bemoan the absence of snow and extol the wonders of snowballs and icicles. After only a couple of days on the road, the Hauna tourists became avid fans of McDonald's and Kentucky Fried Chicken. Having watched Marilyn and Shirley order fast food for several days, Paul was confident that he could order his own food. He got in line first.

"C'n ah he'p yuh?" the girl behind the counter asked.

Shocked, Paul turned to Marilyn, "What language do they speak here?"

"English," Marilyn answered, "but sometimes very different sounding."

Used to the sisters' Hoosier version of American English, the men enjoyed imitating the southern accent whenever they were alone.

Milk shakes and ice-cream bars held special appeal. Joel decided to stash an ice-cream bar in his suitcase for enjoyment later on, requiring an unscheduled side trip to a coin laundry, another first for the men.

Throughout their year in the United States the Hauna team performed nearly two hundred times. They sang in Sepik Iwam, Melanesian Pidgin, and English and shared their testimonies in simple English or with Marilyn translating their words. Tears often filled listeners' eyes when the men explained how God's Talk in their own language had changed lives and made Hauna villagers the brothers and sisters of Christians around the world.

Billy Graham featured the team on a telecast of his Little Rock Crusade in the fall of 1989. Marilyn couldn't help but recall her night in the Oklahoma University stadium in 1965 when she had imagined herself on the platform at a Graham crusade. Now here she was—not to sing a solo, but with her Papua New Guinean cotranslators.

"Who is Billy Graham?" the men asked before the meeting. Marilyn didn't want to worry them before the crusade appearance, so she didn't mention that they would be standing in front of forty-eight thousand that evening, nor did she mention the TV coverage. They would become nervous enough when they entered the stadium.

Jonah brought a touch of humor as he began. "Good evening. My name is Jonah Maiyak. Don't you think that I'm Jonah in the whale. No, this is Jonah from the jungle." The crusade crowd burst into surprised laughter.

"I was saved in 1975," he continued. "I have been working with Marilyn translating the New Testament for the past twenty years. Today I have a verse to say for you. Before I am going to read, I want to say: People like you had the Bible hundreds and hundreds of years ago. But people like us, we didn't. Tonight I am very proud because I have my own Bible, and I can witness to my own people." The audience broke into applause.

"You know, the very first day I held this Bible, my hand was shaking," Jonah continued. "I am very proud because I have been working very hard. Before, I didn't know what to do, but today I understand. I can follow what God wants me to do, the same as you. I am going to read now 1 John 4:7-8."

Jonah read the verses first in Sepik Iwam and then in English. His New Testament contained both. "Dear friends, let us love one another, because love comes from God. Whoever loves is a child of God and knows God. Whoever does not love does not know God, for God is love" (TEV).

Then Paul stepped to the microphone. "Good evening, everyone. My name is Paul Hunney. I was saved in 1969. The very first time Marilyn Laszlo came to Hauna village, I was six years old at that time. When I was seven years old, I accepted Jesus into my life. And, I, also, have been working with her for the past twenty years, translating the Bible into my own language. Tonight I have a verse to share with you, which I memorized. It is found in Luke 6:27. First I am saying it in the Sepik Iwam language and then in English. This verse says: 'But I tell you who hear me: Love your enemies, do good to those who hate you' (TEV).

"Wow, this is a hard verse; how can we handle it?" The audience laughed as they enjoyed the honesty of his question.

"You know, people like you, you can drive ten or fifteen miles without enemies. But we cannot do that. If we do that, we go to the enemy tribe's boundary. Because many years ago our ancestors fought the enemy villages that surrounded us. It is very hard, very difficult for us to help them carry out God's message, to help those people in the jungle, because we were enemies.

"But tonight I want to tell you a little bit about how our ancestors fought against those enemies. This weapon—" he held up a long dagger—"came from the leg bone of one of the largest birds in Papua New Guinea. We call it the cassowary bird. You don't have this animal in this country. It is like an ostrich. This is part of the leg of that bird. And many years ago our ancestors used this weapon to fight against those enemy villages that surrounded us. But we don't use this weapon anymore; this was a long time ago. Today, brothers and sisters, we have a new weapon, which is the Word of God."

A swing through Florida brought the team to Teen Missions Boot Camp on Merritt Island, giving the visitors an opportunity to witness firsthand how teenagers were trained for the kind of services they had rendered in Hauna.

Americans came under the incisive scrutiny of the Hauna translators as they traveled. "Everyone wears a fetish," Jonah said one day, pointing to his wristwatch. "This tells Americans what to do. It pushes, it pulls. It controls everyone's life. It causes lots of fights. It makes people mad at us if we are late. I think it would be better if we threw them away."

Although they averaged about five meetings per week, the eight travelers were able to spend several periods of time at the farm with the Laszlo family near Valparaiso. They took English classes at a local adult education program, amazing their teachers with their zeal to learn and their skill at memorizing.

After practicing on the Laszlo farm, each of the men passed the Indiana driver's license test so they could take turns driving. They loved to joke about not needing a driver's license to use their canoes at home, nor did their canoes require a license plate.

While they disliked American malls, the men loved visiting Kmart and Wal-Mart, always heading for the hardware department to examine the staggering variety of shovels, axes, saws, and hammers. The consensus of opinion was that they wanted to take back to Hauna a McDonald's, a Kentucky Fried Chicken, and either a Wal-Mart or a Kmart hardware section.

Before he toured the U.S. with Marilyn and Shirley, Zechariah had never traveled outside Papua New Guinea. He was encouraged by his tutors at the adult education classes to remain in the U.S. for a few years of further education. He first attended high school in Indiana, and after two and a half years, graduated at the top of his class of three hundred. Accepted at Purdue University, he studied civil engineering for two years, earning an A in most courses. When he returned to Papua New Guinea, he was hired for a top position in a copper mine, a one-day canoe ride from Hauna.

In retrospect, Marilyn and Shirley realized that a year of traveling with almost two hundred speaking engagements had perhaps been too much. The men wearied of the pace, never adjusted to the lifestyle, and suffered increasing bouts of homesickness.

"Your country is great," Paul said, summing up his impressions to Marilyn and Shirley, "but it moves too fast and has too much stuff." Referring to some household knickknacks he added, "And lots of the stuff doesn't even have any function. Knowing Jesus is not about having stuff. There are three things that seem to control most Americans' lives—their watch, stoplights, and money. We don't need any of those things to live in the jungle. Now I have seen America, but I thank God I was born in Papua New Guinea. I am thankful too that so many people here made it possible for you to bring God's Talk to us so we can know God."

TWENTY-TWO

The Word of God Will Last Forever

Everything in this world will someday crumble, whether tropical homes on stilts or huge skyscrapers in the most modern city. But the Word of God in the Sepik Iwam language will last forever.

1990

Numberless birds called out in predawn delight, as if they knew. Frogs were still popping a counterpoint rhythm; the cicadas' shrill song seemed even more clear. An owl hooted, "Good morning." A lone rooster that had survived the pythons and cook pots crowed his daybreak announcement.

Dogs, anxious to get into their masters' canoes for hunting, howled their impatience. Whirlpools in the rivers near Marilyn's house splashed happily as if they knew what was coming.

As she awoke just before the sun crested the horizon, Marilyn could barely contain the excitement already racing through her body. She closed her eyes and let her mind travel back twenty-three tumultuous years to when she and Judy heard their first Sepik Iwam words. Now that language flowed from her mouth and heart, too, like she had never dreamed possible.

Faces of old village friends smiled at her from her memory: Nokiyin, Makapobiya, Sauperi, little baby Marilyn, and so many others.

"Oh, Lord, I certainly hope they are looking down from heaven and watching today's events," she whispered.

As she sat looking out over the village, sipping coffee and waiting for the radio call from Ukarumpa, she saw the smoke filtering up through the thatch roofs. Hauna's people were also awake and huddling around their fires.

Twenty-three years before, there were only fifty-four houses with about four hundred inhabitants; today the population was over eight hundred. Each home in Hauna was decorated for this day, a day she had dreamt about for countless nights. Wild orchids in lavender, pink, and white swayed gently from vines hung at the edges of the roofs. Flaming hibiscus petals splashed color against the backdrop of the rain forest foliage fringing the walls and canoe docks. Sago palm leaves rippled like flags from verandahs, and the pungent perfume of the delicate white and pale yellow frangipani blossom wafted up to greet her nose.

Marilyn recalled the first days of translation with those fourteen little boys and Nokiyin sitting cross-legged on the bark floor of her house. Indelible in her memory was the scene of those boys, now young men, sitting seven on a side of the long translation table. She thanked *Adi Komi* for sparing each of those lives from major illness and death until the process was complete. What a gracious miracle. Six of those translators were now pastors and leaders in the church.

That whole day she lived in anticipation. Late in the afternoon the call came that all had been straining to hear.

Faintly in the distance, then growing in volume, the whole village relayed the message, "The canoe from Ambunti is coming!"

"It's coming, it's coming!"

Hundreds in Hauna hurried to the riverbank carrying fringed palm branches and giant leaves to wave. Marilyn stood at the edge of the hill, scanning the distant horizon of the river to see the canoe.

As the canoe came into sight, a voice in the distance burst out, "The Word of God in my language has arrived!"

Spontaneously others took up the cry: "The Word of God has come!"

An overpowering wave of emotion struck Marilyn by surprise. Joyous, emotional whooping undulated up and down the tributary.

"The Word of God has come!"

Fleeting thoughts of past days—malarial fever, mosquitoes, loneliness, and the incredible frustration—all seemed to burn away just like morning mists in the tropical sun.

"The Word of God has come!"

Was it worth all those years of separation from family? Was it worth all that work translating nearly eight thousand verses?

Oh yes, Lord.

Village children scrambled to help the adults unload the canoes and carry boxes of New Testaments up into Marilyn's house. Hundreds gathered to watch the fourteen translators cut open the boxes.

Each translator took out a copy for himself, holding it gently and tenderly, as if it were a breakable china treasure. As they carefully opened their own copies, tears ran down their cheeks while they rubbed the printed words with their fingers. Rain-forest green had been chosen for the cover color. Etched in gold on the front was a line drawing of a Roman soldier holding up a shield, an item familiar to their culture from their past warring days.

As Marilyn watched through her own tears, she saw Danny go off to a corner to savor the moment, repeating over and over, *"Adi Komi sir yokwo krimir yaikin!"* ("Papa God's carving in our own language!")

They had finished the New Testament. Everything in this world will someday crumble, whether tropical homes on stilts or huge skyscrapers in the most modern city. But the Word of God in the Sepik Iwam language will last forever.

TWENTY-THREE

Hebrews Hall of Faith

*And even when they reached the land God had directed them to,
they lived there by faith—for they were like foreigners,
living in a thatched-roof house.*

Faith. What topic has more definitions yet is more misunderstood than faith? Most people admit that they have at least some, and many long to have more. The author of Hebrews breathes life into dusty definitions by portraying faith in flesh and blood. Biblical heroes of faith, as well as modern-day portrayals, inspire us to continue believing in Jesus.

WHAT IS FAITH? IT IS THE CONFIDENT ASSURANCE THAT WHAT WE HOPE FOR IS GOING TO HAPPEN. IT IS THE EVIDENCE OF THINGS WE CANNOT YET SEE. GOD GAVE HIS APPROVAL TO PEOPLE IN DAYS OF OLD BECAUSE OF THEIR FAITH. BY FAITH WE UNDERSTAND THAT THE ENTIRE UNIVERSE WAS FORMED AT GOD'S COMMAND, THAT WHAT WE NOW SEE DID NOT COME FROM ANYTHING THAT CAN BE SEEN. (HEBREWS 11:1-3, NLT)

It was by faith that Marilyn obeyed when God called her to leave home and go to another land, and so did Judy and later, Shirley. And even when they reached the land God had directed them to, they lived there by faith—for they were like foreigners, living in a thatched-roof house.

And it was by faith that Sauperi, the headman of Hauna, as an old man, spoke about God bringing his people out of darkness. Because of his faith, he gave his own piece of prime land on a hill in the middle of the village for the church and school, a beacon of light. He had faith even when he had no idea where literacy would lead them.

It was by faith that Naoropobiya, who became the village leader and elder after Sauperi's death, was not ashamed to stand firm in support of the outreach and progress of the growing Hauna church.

It was by faith that Nokiyin, the oldest man in the village and leader of his clan, was the first shaman to profess his faith in Jesus. The impact of his faith laid a foundation for the rest of the village to accept Christ.

It was by faith that Makapobiya, the first appointed government official, put his faith in Christ for deliverance from the power of darkness.

It was by faith that aging Kaku and his wife, Yanomok, demonstrated their faith as she lay dying in his arms. Even though she was the first Christian to die in Hauna, she expressed her faith by peacefully saying, "Don't worry, I'm going now to be with Jesus."

It was by faith that Joel, as a young man, refused to be intimidated by the spirits of the jungle, claiming that Jesus' Spirit was more powerful than all the others. He chose to follow God yet drew the respect of all the old village shamans.

It was by faith that Priscilla, Joel's wife, refused to have one of her twin girls killed even though the traditional belief held that the second child was from the devil.

It was by faith that Nigrio, one of the first believers, put

174

his confidence in God and allowed the missionary doctors to amputate his infected leg, saving his life. His faith grew stronger and his testimony more winsome.

It was by faith that the Hauna men built the *Sepik Queen*, to provide safer travel up and down the Sepik River for literacy and evangelistic outreaches. Even though they had never seen steel float, they continued to work conscientiously side-by-side with the visiting boat makers.

By faith, fourteen boys stood with Marilyn until the entire New Testament was completed. Through their faith and the grace of God, not one became seriously ill or died until after the translation was published.

It was by their faith that Christina, Ranu, Betty, Catherine, Veronica, Priscilla, and Sarah helped in countless ways to speed the translation process. The list of hardworking women who helped would take pages to inventory.

How much more can be said? It would take too long to recount the story of faith of each Hauna Christian who helped with the translation and of all the literacy instructors who faithfully taught classes in Hauna when reading had never before been part of the culture.

All of these people, and so many others not mentioned in this book, received God's approval because of their faith; yet many of them did not live to hold the printed copy of the Sepik Iwam New Testament in their own hands.

THEREFORE, SINCE WE ARE SURROUNDED BY SUCH A HUGE CROWD OF WITNESSES TO THE LIFE OF FAITH, LET US STRIP OFF EVERY WEIGHT THAT SLOWS US DOWN, ESPECIALLY THE SIN THAT SO EASILY HINDERS OUR PROGRESS. AND LET US RUN WITH ENDURANCE THE RACE THAT GOD HAS SET BEFORE US. WE DO THIS BY KEEPING OUR EYES ON JESUS, ON WHOM OUR FAITH DEPENDS FROM START TO FINISH. (HEBREWS 12:1-2, NLT)

EPILOGUE

How does it work?
How can the Bible be translated into languages around
the world and impact the lives it touches?

How is it that Christianity "works" in every culture and
language? Because God created them in the first place! God
created each person with the ability to reach out and accept
his love and grace when clearly presented with the gospel.

How does it work? How did God use an average Midwest
farm girl to bring his Talk to a preliterate society? How did
he keep her there? Why does God use each of us? He uses us
to prove his power in our weakness. Faced with a task too
huge and impossible for us, despair develops when we forget that the work is his, that we are merely cooperating
within his grand design.

Praise God, he also calls brilliant linguists into ministry
who consult with those of us less astute in the technical
areas while completing their own translations. Praise God
for skillful mechanics who keep machines and engines running and pilots who fly aircraft to out-of-the-way places like
Hauna. How can I ever thank all the support workers—
administrators, bookkeepers, printers, secretaries, teachers,
writers, etc.—in Papua New Guinea and in the U.S., who
have stayed at their jobs to take care of the "behind-the-
scenes" details? My list of thanks extends to all the loyal

prayer and financial partners who have formed the foundation of strength vital to the Sepik Iwam program.

I thank God for my faithful Sepik Iwam neighbors and coworkers, who opened their throats to me. I have been blessed to have lived and worked alongside you for over twenty years.

How does it work? How can a shaman become a New Testament translator? How can preteen boys, born in the rain forest of Papua New Guinea, teach literacy classes and also become Bible translators and eventually preach sermons to Americans?

When Jesus said, "Go into all the world and preach the gospel," he did not give us an impossible task, no matter where we go in this world. It is possible, no matter how overwhelming it sounds, because he goes with us.

It is a mission that is possible!

Marilyn Laszlo
April 1998

Luci Brockway Tumas and her husband, John, raised their two children, Matt and Kristi, in Papua New Guinea, spending fifteen years at Ukarumpa, the main center for the Summer Institute of Linguistics (sister organization of Wycliffe Bible Translators). Throughout her years at Ukarumpa, Luci helped in various offices and taught music. The last six years she directed a teen evangelistic tour choir and worked as a writer in the Media Services Department. Now living in Fort Wayne, Indiana, John heads the SIL Accounting Office for several SIL entities in Africa, and Luci writes for various Wycliffe publications.

Wycliffe Bible Translators believe the Bible is God's message for everyone and that the most effective means of bringing it to people is in the recipients' mother tongue. They have completed New Testament translations in nearly five hundred languages spoken by over 30 million people.

Wycliffe's fifty-three hundred members come from the U.S. and forty-five other countries. They are at work in more than one thousand languages in over seventy countries— with small tribes in some of the most remote locations on earth, as well as in modern cities with large refugee populations. Sometimes they work where the gospel has never been heard before. In other areas they work in partnership with local churches or national Bible translation organizations. Many Wycliffe members work behind the scenes flying or fixing airplanes, surveying languages, purchasing supplies, teaching missionaries' children, arranging for visas, managing computer networks, and doing hundreds of jobs that help the work of Bible translation.

The task of reaching people of every language is far from complete. Of the world's 6,703 living languages, work is going on in over 1,000. Another 900 have definite translation needs, but there aren't enough translators to do the work. Surveying needs to be done in another 2,000 languages to determine their needs.

If you are interested in learning more about Wycliffe Bible Translators and how you can become involved

Visit Wycliffe's Web site: www.wycliffe.org
Send E-mail to info.usa@wycliffe.org
Call 1-800-992-5433 or
Write to Wycliffe Bible Translators, P.O. Box 2727, Huntington Beach, CA 92647

Maybe God is calling you to be part of the team!